THE NETHERLANDS

PROMETHEUS

THE

NETHERLANDS

A practical Guide for the Foreigner
and
a Mirror for the Dutch

2001
Prometheus/NRC Handelsblad
Amsterdam/Rotterdam

First edition April 2001
Second edition May 2001
Third edition September 2001

This book has been translated by Sam Garrett and Rémy Chavannes,
with the exception of the contributions by Marc Chavannes, Sarah Hart,
Titia Ketelaar and Ethel Portnoy, which were written directly in English.

ISBN 90 5333 986 8

Table of contents

Introduction

Half of the Netherlands, one of the most densely populated countries in the world, lies below sea level. Here soft drugs are prohibited, but their sale is tolerated. Every two years, half the population dresses in orange in anticipation of the national football team's success in an international tournament – despite the fact that, according to the Dutch, nationalism tends to occur only beyond the country's borders.

A curious country. It is both rich and prosperous, yet around one million of its potential employees are deemed unfit to work. The Dutch see themselves as modern and cosmopolitan, they have an opinion about everything, yet a discussion about the monarchy will hardly get off the ground. They behave with openness and tolerance towards foreigners, but only on condition that those foreigners know how to fit in. They are also keen to assimilate other languages, if occasionally in rather mutilated form, into their official dictionary, as long as those words happen to be English (or American). The Dutch are proud of their liberal and innovative art climate, have a poorly developed memory when it comes to their national history, and are always curious as to what foreigners think of them.

Hence this book. So that foreigners can get to know more about the Dutch and their character. About the Netherlands and its internationally renowned 'polder model', or 'Dutch model': the eternal – and generally successful – endeavour to reach a consensus between political parties and between employers and trade unions. This book allows foreigners to taste a country that is the Mecca of the untranslatable word, *gedogen*, meaning 'to consciously allow that which is forbidden'.

The Netherlands has been written by editors and staff of the NRC *Handelsblad*, a national evening newspaper, and by guest writers. The articles also include short news items on typical Dutch subjects from NRC *Handelsblad*. This book is meant for foreigners who want to understand more about this country, and for Dutch people who are not afraid to look in the mirror, and who occasionally like to read something about themselves in another language.

John Kroon

MPS LEAK INFORMATION

THE HAGUE. **Prime Minister Kok has reacted angrily to reports that a number of MPs have leaked details of discussions with Queen Beatrix. Speaking after the cabinet's weekly meeting, Mr Kok emphasised that such discussions with the Queen can only prove useful if they remain confidential.**
According to the leaks, the Queen was concerned about the increasing lack of security in society, and about the empty prison cells.

THE DUTCH MODEL (1)

The 'Dutch model', or 'Polder Model', is famous in and beyond Europe. It stands for: discussion for as long as it takes to reach an agreement. For not making a decision until there is a feeling of general consensus. For practical action if there is no room for a viewpoint based on principles. For a country with republican traits, which nevertheless has a monarchy.

A modern queen
and other contradictions

Marc Chavannes

Once upon a time there was a King, who was really a Queen. She lived in a palace filled, even unto the ceilings, with beautiful paintings by the old masters. In fact, She was a bit of an artist Herself, a sculptor of sorts. She adored worKing with clay. When one came to dinner at the palace, She needed only little encouragement to show Her entire art collection and, after a bit of prodding, Her own work as well.

She was a jack-of-all-trades, with a good head on Her shoulders. She had complete mastery over even the minutest Matters of State. You name it, and She could give you the figures. All those who counted in the Kingdom admired Her a great deal for Her diligence and sheer command of the facts. The Constitution was the novel of Her life.

Which is why She didn't see the danger looming ahead. The Crown seemed beyond dispute to Her, but alas it was in for a curious mixture of Opposition and Oblivion. As the chorus in this unfolding drama had it: 'O King-Queen, beware! Thy staunchest supporters in their heart of hearts deem thee a Hint of a Hindrance for behaving like a King! The crowd wants a heart, no head on top!'

Yet 'twas to no avail. For She was too happily-hard-working not to be a trifle conceited. You know how it is; the trouble with the very talented can be their failure to see ordinary folk. Her mother, the previous Queen, had been a granny to the millions. That had worked well. But nobody openly blamed this Queen. She really was a most dedicated King.

Nobody dared to doubt Her application. She had even made a habit of visiting Her subjects in their humble settlements around the country; a dream that came true every year, when the populace was invited to celebrate Her birthday. It was not Her real birthday, of course. Her private birthday was another occasion altogether. Then She preferred to have a ball with Her family and friends on Her estate in Italy.

This King (who was really a Queen) lived in a densely populated parKing lot by the sea. She had ruled it for twenty years now, but wouldn't hear of abdication – She was just getting the hang of it. The people were careful enough to confirm to Her each morning that She was a very able King, but some people dared to say to each other that perhaps Her hairdo was becoming a bit old hat.

Worse yet, others started telling tales of Her involvement in Matters That Mattered. She had opposed the former

---

D66 LEADER WANTS TO MODERNISE MONARCHY

THE HAGUE. **Thom de Graaf, leader of junior coalition party D66, has called for a drastic modernisation of the monarchy. The hereditary head of state should no longer be part of the government, no longer be involved in cabinet formations and should resign as Chairman of the Council of State. De Graaf expects a change of monarch within the next eight years. He argues that this period should be used to hold a public debate and prepare changes to the Constitution, a process that generally takes at least four years.**

Prime Minister's next-in-line because he was a Christian Democrat and he had seen no other choice but to become a building contractor. When, for example, a Centre-Left government had come to power, one commentator suggested, it had shown Her hand. The King was also rumoured to have had an ambassador transferred to a faraway nation, because he had spoken openly of the King's son.

It was, in fact, the most public of secrets that this King had a son. Three sons in fact, but the two ablest of them pursued careers in ordinary life, earning their own money and so forth. This Crown Son, therefore, had to be nurtured with great care. He was the only one willing to take on 'The Job', as the Royals referred to Mother's High Calling.

The Crown Son was not as gifted as his mother, the King. The oldest university in the land had given him a degree in Royalty only to save the professors the trouble of having to explain even the simplest material to Him, over and over again. Subsequently, He was awarded a position on the International Olympic Committee, strictly on merit of course.

As He was getting on for Thirty-Something, it occurred to all that most boys His age had relationships. And some of them even found a partner. Now you probably know that the dating and mating habits of Royals is the most dramatically underresearched subject in all of biochemistry. Their genetic code being very different from ours, there is of course a severe lack of control groups for representative lab work. The monarchy is a great subject for popular research, but even the scientists of Man and Mind have not yet seized this opportunity. But then, they have never had a way with rare species. Only children's literature has ever exhibited a full-blown interest in the monarchy.

Anyway, no one in the Kingdom by the Sea seemed to realise that the stability at the Summit of State was extremely fragile. With a King whose image was eroding, and a Crown Son in need of an officially approved playmate, a tiny industrial accident could spark off a constitutional crisis. And worst of all, the burghers seemed to be entirely indifferent. Many thought that the court was a national fairy tale, something one could order for delivery, like a pizza, whenever the appetite arose: for the annual opening of Parliament or to perform a nice television wedding, when the TV guide was low on soccer and tennis.

To be frank, however, the Parkingdom by the Sea had never really taken the trouble to go after the Court's Secrets, perhaps because they assumed there were none. Short of memory they were, these citizens, for most Parkings in the last century or two had led strange lives, with more than one man's helping of frustration. They had often suffered from a lack of serious occupation, and had compensated by going after other people's wives – not very safe in those days. A more recent prince consort had even enlisted an American aircraft company to finance his jet-set lifestyle. It can hardly be denied: Royal Women had saved the throne from their Male Companions over and over again. Kings tended to be sillier than Queens, at least in this Queendom by the Sea.

Meanwhile, the Royal Court had failed to count its blessings. The country had always sported a rather friendly and forgetful press, which waited for all news to be confirmed by official sources. And the sources close to the palace usually said there *was* no news, unless it spilled over the royal doormat and tumbled down the five steps leading to the cobblestone drive.

Now, it is important that you realise that all this is history. Things have changed dramatically of late. For a start, the King invited a busload of hacks for drinks and Confidential Observations. For example, She confided to them that it was not She, but Lies that ruled the land. That sounded interesting to the scribes at hand. 'Maybe that's News', one mumbled, and wearily they put aside their glasses of Château Comme Si wine.

'Could you please repeat that, Your Majesty?' She had rehearsed this diatribe so often over muffins and morning coffee, in fact throughout the day and even unto the moment that She and Her Husband brushed Their Golden Teeth, that She easily improvised an indictment of the press that could not possibly be kept out of print.

The Chief Hack, who in daily life edited the People's Paper, tried to restrain his young colleagues from doing their duties. But as these things often go, the cub reporters felt only encouraged by the official attention, and wrote beautiful stories detailing the King's misgivings.

Now everybody knew that She felt misunderstood, unappreciated and, in fact, unloved. She also let it be known that in the old days, when a newspaper report displeased the Palace, She had merely to pick up the phone and call the press barons. The next day She would read a very pleasing half-page-write-up. Ah, those were the days! Post-modern times may be fun in literature, but not in the realm of royalty.

So where did we stand with this King who Queened over Her citizens? Would things automatically get better once Her reputedly good humoured son, the Crown Son, took over The Job? Or was the concept in need of a complete and dramatic overhaul? Would only a King.dot.com solution save the Queen?

To add insult to injury, the amiable Son of a Queen had found the Woman of his Dreams. That, at least, was what the People's Paper reported, giving away Her name. The loudest paper on the ParKing Lot published a picture of her, taken from the back, which unfortunately turned out not to be of her but of someone else. It was correct, though, in reporting that her father had been a dictator's assistant in Latin America.

People started imagining the Royal Wedding Day: this retired executioner's accomplice waving his washed hands, standing on the palace steps beside the monarch. Would the fans remain unperturbed and wave their little flags, as usual? Or would they shy away from the fireworks and festivities after all? A situation that might drag the Queen into the politics of ultra-right-wing Latino landownership.

Some astute constitutionalists claimed that any parliament worth its salt would demand that the young Queen-to-be excommunicate her father, the Colonel's comrade in evil. What a predicament for a loving daughter! Oh, and by the way, she was a Roman Catholic; not exactly the house religion of the Dynasty by the Sea. But who cared? When a picture turned up that actually was of her, she looked nice enough.

Then the Royal Henhouse was startled once more by the Declaration of Independence of the youngest Turk in the Sea-Kingdom's political nobility. On behalf of the Party To End All Parties he said that the King should not be part of government, but the Head of State would not be a figurehead either. And he added, 'I love the King; let's discuss the options for a more perfect democracy in which She has no power whatsoever!'

Nobody understood exactly how that would work out. But that didn't prevent most courtiers from speaking their minds. A Liberal lackey said that the Young Turk's words lacked 'That Orange Glow'. You must know that the Kings had adopted the orange as their logo, long before a local computer firm in Silicon Valley had adopted the apple. But now even the orange looked rather sour and bitten.

Again, the usual political hanky-panky bespoke a profound rift running straight through the ParKing Lot People. On the one hand, there were the indifferent, who thought that the Court was a nice charade that provided them with the occasional free meal and a day off. And, on the other, one could also observe the indifferent who loved to engage in Fundamental Debate, as long as it was inconsequential.

Both constituencies had a field day. The Orangists repeated ad nauseam that the King was such a wonderful Queen. The republicans were caught unawares. They had been banking on a few more drinks, and a meeting or two, before their time would come. In the ensuing vacuum, the Arch-Wisemen discovered a niche market with pleas for cautious calm.

What, you may well wonder, did the People make of all this? The opinion polls found that 72 percent of the People said it was fine with them to have a King who wielded political influence. And 58 percent would even allow the King to venture forth freely with Her opinions on political matters.

In short, about two thirds of the King's burghers didn't trust Democracy, or themselves for that matter. They didn't care about logic. They felt that having a King was 'nice'. Maybe they realised that national power was leaking away to the Slightly-United States of Europe. So the King was becoming more like a Memorial to National Unity. Hadn't She spoken out courageously against the German Invader during World War II?

Ah, for here we hit upon the joint territory of the two top taboos in the Kingdom by the Shallow Sea: the War Memory and the House of the Oranges. Doomed is he or she who defies the notion of inherent pride embodied by these two institutions. They symbolise what is sturdy and common in a people with a very flimsy sense of history. Take away these largely fictitious elements and the backdrop runs the risk of falling over, to reveal a flat and empty stage.

National Unity is the one and only lasting task for a modern King. He or She who forgets this truism, and starts reading White Papers and bills before parliament, gets into trouble. Forming an opinion is an unnecessary risk. In modern times, the King is there to avoid having a humdrum elected president. You need someone to man the palace. Above the fray, if at all possible.

The relevant literature reports no hereditary aptitude for the job of King. But the dna people will find it. For the time being, it is a gamble. So if the present Crown Son proves to be a jolly good chap and a swinging soccer fan, He will make a great King. Especially with a national team that somehow manages to snatch defeat from the jaws of victory by missing five out of six penalties in international tournaments. National Unity is a more down-to-earth affair than most people realise.

The Monarchy has always been a matter of theatre. Deep down, every King is begging his people for clemency, as King Lear did when his time was up:

MÁXIMA TO GET HER OWN PERFUME LINE

ROTTERDAM. **Perfume company Royal Sanders has developed a range of perfumes around** *Máxima* **Zorreguieta, the girlfriend of Dutch Crown Prince Willem-Alexander. Called** *Máxima*, **the range will include perfume, shower gel and body lotion. The company hopes to begin advance sales of Máxima products soon. They will only become available if and when Willem-Alexander and Máxima announce their engagement.**

You must bear with me:
Pray you now, forget and forgive: I am old and foolish.

Before those final words were uttered, Lear's dear Fool had offered practical advice, with the words:

He that has and a little tiny wit
With hey, ho, the wind and the rain,
Must make content with his fortunes fit,
For the rain it raineth every day.

Marc Chavannes is correspondent in the United States for NRC *Handelsblad.*

The Netherlands has been a constitutional monarchy since 1815. In the words of the Constitution: 'The Head of State is immune, the Ministers are responsible.' So the Ministers, and not the King, shall be responsible for acts of government.

During the Second World War, Queen Wilhelmina, widow of the German-born Prince Hendrik, escaped to London, from where She broadcast words of encouragement to Her subjects under Nazi occupation. She abdicated in 1948 and was succeeded by Her daughter Queen Juliana (married to the German Prince Bernhard), who in Her turn turned over the throne in 1980 to Her daughter Queen Beatrix (married to the German Claus von Amsberg, who was made a Prince). The eldest son of the current royal couple is Willem-Alexander.

THE DUTCH AND THEIR MORES

Crowded together on their small patch of land are the almost 16 million Dutch. They are becoming increasingly well off, but also less healthy. It is a country full of sinners and folklore, say the foreigners. But is this really the case? Reflections on the Dutch, their character and customs.

The traffic jam as national symbol

H.J.A. Hofland

'The traffic jams began early today. At four o'clock this afternoon, there was a total of 127 kilometres of cars bumper-to-bumper on the Dutch roads,' said the girl from the ANWB-head office. It was June 14 in the year 2000, a heavily overcast day. The humiliating conclusion of the European football championships was already too far behind for anyone but the historians to even think about. The Holland Festival was in full swing. The only thing really bothering the Dutch was that phenomenon which has, since human memory, always been an inexhaustible source of conversation, and which was now again the topic of the day: the rain. This year, once again, 'summer just didn't want to happen'. And to makes things worse, there were 127 kilometres of traffic jams. The girl from the ANWB was an old hand on the subject, but today she was audibly surprised. She actually seemed to enjoy it, the announcement of a new record. She spoke flawless 'Polder Dutch' as the youngest twist on our mother tongue has been dubbed by Dr Jan Stroop; the hyper-Dutch, that with its special R, does have a certain carefree quality. No wonder she sounded so cheerful. For here lies the very heart of the Dutch paradox. As the new century begins, the nation changes very quickly... and yet remains the same. We are a blessed folk. The Central Planning Office has just calculated that our economic growth this year will be stronger than even the optimists had predicted: 4.7 percent. Consumption per family is increasing by 4.6 percent. Employment has risen yet again. The number of millionaires is growing steadily; at the beginning of the new millennium there were, for the first time, more than 200,000 of them. Top salaries have risen by 13 percent. And passenger-vehicle sales are unstoppable; in the last two years, their numbers have increased by more than a million. At the same time, we are drinking more and more beer. The Dutch prefer the special beers, which are also the more expensive ones. Per head of the population in 1999, they swilled almost 90 litres of beer and almost the same quantity of soft drinks. The consumption of wine has increased by almost a quarter; milk, however, is losing popularity (now under 70 litres). All in all, who wouldn't want to live in such a country? Our cabinet ministers visibly strain to find a humanitarian way to stem the ever-increasing flow of refugees – political, economic or otherwise – crossing our borders each year. Young people are optimistic: more and more children are being born. The old are hardly sombre: their life-expectancy is rising. Who would choose not to live in a country like this? In the first year of this new century, we shall greet the 16 millionth Dutch person.

The people are changing. Less than ten years ago, most young Dutch people would have preferred a steady job with a chance of promotion and a systematic, resolute building up of their pension. Young people had become more adventurous long before this, but this spirit of mobility had not expressed itself on the job market. Only at the end of the Cold War, with the dawning of the free-market, did the revolution gain momentum. The phenomenon which in America is called the 'rat-race' had reached our country. It rapidly became so serious that the government decided it was time to do something about it. The former minister of the environment, Mrs. Margreet de Boer, actually made a public appeal to 'de-haste'. Here we see the first example of the way in which we always remain true to ourselves: by formulating good intentions that are never followed up, except in the dictionary.

The minister had enriched the language, but the rush only became more serious. Haste is a result of work pressure. One encounters more work pressure when one's goal is to keep up, to climb as high as possible on the ladder of society and to earn more.

But why do people want that? Silly question. In order to enjoy their lives even more, of course. There are more stimulants and pleasure paraphernalia available to the Dutch than ever before in the history of our Fatherland. Eating a magic mushroom, popping a pill, scoring a line is all about enjoyment. You can buy your mushrooms at a 'smart shop' where the proprietor has a certificate. Yet beware! Only those with a certificate bear the official seal of approval. Only when you buy here do you know that you are about to ingest the very best. And accept no substitutes: take only certified XTC.

Just enjoy! Use your mobile in the tram, race through the city on your scooter on a Saturday afternoon with your radio on loud: that's enjoyment... Fun-shopping!

Transporting your first child in a speedy three-wheel buggy: don't tell me that's no fun! Then home again (mortgage of three hundred thousand or even six, who cares?) to slip a CD of *Kunst der Fuge* into the hi-fi: double enjoyment! Discussing the holiday bungalow in Aruba: an advance on future enjoyment. Balancing your bankbook, you discover that liquidity is getting a bit tight... so you buy a ticket for the Postcode Lottery. And enjoy hoping. And if you don't believe in luck: just work harder. Then that evening, to soothe the jangled nerves, you watch something on a fun-channel. After all, that's a form of enjoyment too. Besides, if that doesn't work, you always have recourse to the old Dutch expressions that translate literally as: 'Don't lift too much hay on your fork' or 'The bow cannot always be drawn'.

In our country, nothing remains un-investigated. Recent figures (from a study by Intromart, July 2000) show that 78 percent of all Dutch people find 'work pressure to be the disease of our times'; 43 percent of the working population regularly works too hard, and 10 percent is suffering from burnout. The first symptoms are insomnia, irritability, and outbursts of irrational anger; after all this, the stage of actual stress begins. Complicated perhaps by a mouse-arm or other complaints caused by Repetitive Strain Injury (RSI). Intestinal ailments are also on the increase. In the worst of cases, ending with burnout. The patient is convinced that 'everything is going wrong', he breaks down and ends up there where he most feared ending up: on the unpaved shoulder of society. Teachers, doctors and policemen run the greatest risk of burnout. The Dutch working population totals 7.1 million; the early summer of 2000 saw 924,000 of them in the 'WAO': in other words, sick at home.

About half a century ago, there was a sociologist teaching at the State University of Groningen by the name of Professor Dr P.J. Bouman. And he was more than simply an erudite

---

BANK CALLS FOR HOMELESS TO BE GIVEN ACCOUNTS

AMSTERDAM. **The Dutch Central Bank is urging high street banks to be more helpful and flexible with the growing number of homeless people unable to get a bank account. Although it has no legal powers to force banks to open accounts, its role as official regulator of the banking sector will ensure that banks are inclined to listen. The issue was raised with the Central Bank by the Salvation Army, which has thousands of clients who are unable to get their own bank account because they have too many debts or are likely to cause problems.**

scholar; he also had sociological intuition. At that time, the late Fifties, he toyed with the idea of writing an essay that would be called: The Sociology of the Dutch Shift. At that time there were still only II million of us. We would do well, he said, to bear in mind the behavioural shift seen among higher mammals when too many of them are crowded together in too small a space. They become nervous, they start biting each other and, not uncommonly, themselves (Bouman's tone was rather sombre). In the last few years, however, I have often thought back on Bouman's sociology of change.

Yet things have gone differently than he expected: better, in one way at least, and worse in others. Today, sixteen million of us still share almost the same surface area. But the Dutch of half a century ago were different from those today. We have become notably more affluent and, above all, much more flexible; what we call 'social discipline', however, is not what it used to be – to put it mildly and without grousing. That, too, is a fact of daily life. A simple calculation shows that the chances that two Dutch people will get in each other's way in one way or another – physically, with their personal habits, their careers, with the sounds which accompany their existence – have become infinitely greater. Is it then any less than self-evident that we occasionally behave like Professor Bouman's higher mammals? This change in national behaviour is the denominator of all changes. In New York I recently spoke to someone who was born and bred there. The pace of public life in Manhattan is, I would estimate, about two times higher than ours. Yet he enjoyed the peace he found when he went home again. 'You guys are so frenetic,' he said.

The girl from the ANWB traffic control centre had 127 kilometres of traffic jams to announce. The day before it had been perhaps 83 or 42 kilometres, but now that everyone was back from their holidays, we could get a new record of 132 kilometres or more. This is the aspect of the Netherlands which does not change. We identify the big issues, we do research, committees do all they can to find a solution, and after that there are opportunities for public comment, followed by broad collective discussions. None of this solves the issue. On the contrary. Growth is then simply tolerated, and the time gained in this way is used for reconsideration. Meanwhile, the government and political parties cherish the (vain) hope that the problem will solve itself. Out of a system of tolerance (a deceptive attempt to keep all parties on friendly terms) and reconsideration (the result: even greater befuddlement than before), stagnation arises. The greatest pool of national stagnation to date has formed around Schiphol Airport. Another, similar stagnation of national scale is caused by the problem of the High Speed Train Line. The third is that with the 'drugs issue' at its core, which elicits tragicomedy after tragicomedy, without coming one step closer to a solution. The traffic reports illustrate the essence of Dutch stagnation; the traffic-jam itself is its symbol.

The Netherlands: a magnificent country. The Dutch nationality is an enviable one. But the rapid changing of the Dutch clashes each and every day with the stagnation they have built into their system. From this arise the disadvantages which, at the beginning of this century, are simply part of being Dutch.

Journalist and writer H.J.A. Hofland has worked for NRC *Handelsblad* (formerly *Algemeen Handelsblad*) since 1953, mostly as a commentator and a columnist.

'Don't kill me, doctor!'

STEREOTYPES ABOUT THE DUTCH

Titia Ketelaar

Try to characterise a Dutchman, and most non-Dutch will give you the story of the little boy with his finger in the dike: blond hair, blue eyes, a pair of puffy trousers and, of course, the inevitable clogs. In the background there is a windmill and, preferably, some tulips.

If this is not the picture that is portrayed, it will, no doubt, be of the 'other' Dutchman: the sex-crazed, drug-using advocate of free abortion and euthanasia, extremely tolerant of others and with a liberal attitude towards everything that is banned in other countries.

And no wonder this image of the Dutch exists. A look at the foreign press provides excellent insight into what other nations think: *The Daily Telegraph*, April 2000, 'Crime gangs feed on Dutch coffee shops', *The Guardian*, January 1999: 'Amsterdam brothels go legit', *The Daily Telegraph*, October 1999: 'Dutch carry cards that say: Don't kill me doctor!'

Needless to say, the Dutch are none too pleased with this image. A 1993 study by the Dutch Ministry of Economics and the Dutch Tourist Board found that potential tourists considered the Netherlands, and particularly Amsterdam, to be unsafe and dirty. The antidote was to use the 'friendly' Dutch image: lots of tulips and clogs and windmills – one stereotype to counter another. This campaign seems to have helped. A study by the Ministry of Foreign Affairs in November 2000, concluded that those unknown with the Netherlands, associate the country with precisely those symbols.

'There must be some truth to the stereotypes if people from different countries all think alike about one nation,' says Professor Nico Wilterdink from the University of Amsterdam. He has conducted extensive research on national stereotypes, and has found that thinking in stereotypes is necessary for people to order the world: to distinguish 'us' from 'them'.

'Stereotypes are partly based on the truth, but they are also simplifications and generalisations. For example, the Dutch policy with regard to drugs stands out internationally. This leads to the generalisation that the Dutch are extremely tolerant for accepting the policy, which then becomes "all Dutch are on drugs" or something similar.' Wilterdink calls it 'psychologising politics'.

So what do foreigners living in the Netherlands think of its inhabitants? Are the 'cloggies' what we expect them to be? The general comment seems to be that 'image isn't everything'. Not surprisingly, they discover not all the Dutch are on drugs, and that only an estimated 5000 out of 16 million Dutch people actually wear clogs.

'When you are in this country for longer than just a short stay, you realise that their famous tolerance is based on

---

DUTCH LIKE VOLUNTEER WORK

AMSTERDAM. **The number of volunteer workers in the Netherlands is among the highest in the world. According to a report by the Office of Social and Cultural Planning (scp), the willingness of people to work for altruistic motives or idealistic causes has actually increased during the past decades.**

clichés,' says South African Russel Bark, who has lived in The Hague for a year. 'They keep telling me how wrong apartheid is, but if you hear them talking about the Surinamese or the Moroccans, well, they are not as tolerant as they believe themselves to be.'

He also finds the country less liberal, and too organised: 'There's no spontaneity, there are too many rules, and the Dutch are too focused on money. The first thing they ask is: *Wat kost het?* In the supermarket they look at cents. Does it matter if something costs 4.95 guilders or 4.99 guilders?'

Helmut Hetzel, Benelux-correspondent for the German newspaper *Die Welt* for more than ten years, finds the Dutch to be 'friendly' and 'surprisingly humorous', but often 'meddlesome'. 'The famous Dutch index finger does exist. They feel a kind of moral superiority towards other nations, and cannot resist telling them that something in their home-country should be different.'

Hetzel also misses profound conversations, especially in public and political debate. 'As a German, I notice that in Holland you don't discuss. Or you do, but without depth. That is no coincidence: the Dutch are not a nation of philosophers, like the Germans are. They have only had Spinoza, but he came from Portugal. Holland is more a nation of painters, lawyers and writers. And, of course, a nation of merchants.'

If the existing stereotypes are wide of the mark, it might be time to try and portray the country in a different way. The question is how? If the tulips, windmills and clogs – and the liberal attitude towards drugs, sex, abortion and euthanasia – are not the true Dutch image, then what is?

Titia Ketelaar is an editor at NRC *Handelsblad*.

Meet the chilly, passionate Dutch

Han van der Horst

In the summer, one look at the commuter trains connecting the major cities of the Netherlands is enough to tell us that a large part of the population has gone abroad. No need for artful pushing and shoving to get a seat. The Dutch have, as usual, dispersed to their holiday hideouts. They will, of course, be back in the second half of August, because these days the school authorities tend to get extremely upset if children miss a day of school.

The Netherlands is a well-ordered nation, and one that places a premium on standing by an agreement. In fact, even laws and obligations are cast in the language of an agreement. A few years ago a television documentary showed a prison director treating one of his guests to fourteen days withdrawal of privileges for drug abuse, only to finish by saying, quite gently: Agreed?

The Dutchmen – and women – who you will meet abroad in the summer have extricated themselves from this system of agreement for a few weeks. When they come back, they will spend their meagre lunch breaks – half an hour is standard – waxing lyrical about the incomparable atmosphere they encountered while on holiday in your country. Once over the border, the pocket diary had ceased to exert its inexorable influence over their daily life.

The Dutch spend most of their day keeping appointments. It is not unusual for them to be asked for a business meeting at ten past one, rather than at one o'clock or twelve thirty. Even their evenings are organised along these lines. No one is surprised to find two old friends inspecting their diaries, only to come to the conclusion that the first suitable date for a dinner appointment is in three weeks' time. Appointments are made well in advance, because once they have been made, it is 'not done' to change them.

And once back from his holiday, the Dutchman will affectionately remember the little train he took, chugging lazily from village to village through your beautiful countryside, only to get extremely agitated about the fact that Dutch express trains sometimes have delays of up to fifteen minutes.

During their lunch breaks, the Dutch will also speak fondly of the real friendship that they discovered abroad. Of course, they are confusing the forging of ties of friendship with the cordiality which you, as a result of your decent upbringing, extend to foreigners. All this is due to a number of fundamental characteristics of Dutch society, which cause the average Dutchman to maintain a strict distinction between the private and the public sphere. Partly for this reason, many employees of the multinational Unilever regard a posting to the Netherlands as a punishment.

Those sent there are thrown into a diary-driven environment in which everyone rushes out of the office after work, rather than sharing a drink with their colleagues. The people seem cold and reserved, without any real interest in each other. In reality, however, the Dutch are very keen on friendship. As far as they are concerned, loneliness is the worst fate that can befall a human being. Here, even socio-economic phenomena such as poverty or unemployment are defined in terms of social exclusion.

Debate about those at the bottom of the social ladder concentrates on the fact that those earning least have too little income to maintain a normal social life. This may seem a paradox, but it isn't.

When it comes right down to it, the Netherlands has

always been very divided. In its heyday, the epoch of Rembrandt and Johannes Vermeer, the country was no more than a union of sovereign states, organised in turn along federal lines. The only way to achieve anything in Dutch society is to leave your fellow human beings to themselves as much as possible, while trying your utmost to bring about compromises on the rare occasions when meeting and co-operation are inevitable.

The Netherlands is not a country where boasters do well. In general, they quickly find themselves confronted with a broad coalition of enemies. The Dutch people is still made up of minorities and sub-cultures who want to be left alone as much as possible. But to achieve that, co-operation is required at many levels. This principle is illustrated by the dictum 'accept others as they are'.

The Dutch seek to control their lives through countless appointments and meetings. Personal friendships, however, sometimes upset this subtle and inbred process, and that is precisely why the Dutch make such a sharp distinction between professional networks and personal relationships. Various forms of modern discourse even see marriage as little more than a negotiating relationship. This also explains why the Dutch can at first appear to be so cold and casual, and why they are so easily impressed by the ordinary warmth of your country.

Something else may have struck you as well: the Dutch have no manners. At home they keep up the fiction of equality, because without it the entire system of compromise collapses. The 60s witnessed a thorough reappraisal of basic principles, which taught them to think that all forms of decorum are nonsense. Thus they have excelled over the last twenty-five years in their peculiar form of blunt informality, which makes them descend upon restaurant terraces wearing bermuda shorts, while the people of your city would dress for dinner.

The Netherlands has long been a trading nation, with widespread international contacts. As a result, the Dutch often regard themselves as cosmopolitan. They are fairly impressed by their knowledge of foreign languages. However, a real cosmopolitan would know that only a Chinese gentleman can retain his dignity while wearing shorts, for the simple reason that a Chinese gentleman retains his dignity in all circumstances.

And not only that. As it turns out, the Dutch have opinions they simply cannot keep to themselves. They even seem to have outspoken preferences for particular politicians in your country. Even without being asked, they offer advice on how your society might be better organised. But why? They seem such reserved people. Ah, but you see, you're a Friend now. And when they're among friends there are no business issues at stake, so they don't need to be careful. They tell it like they think it is, sorting the boys from the men and the sheep from the goats. Because it doesn't matter when they're among friends, and, provided that they're accepted for what they are, there's nothing they like more than to spout their wisdom – in no uncertain terms – in a friendly environment.

The Dutch reveal themselves to be determined polemicists who don't shy away from confrontation. They mean no harm, they go at it in precisely the same way at family parties, which are usually in honour of someone's birthday. As long as it doesn't get personal, for they wouldn't stand for a personal attack on themselves either. They will complain about happenstance in the fiercest of terms, until the publican finally stops filling their glasses.

So just nod at them encouragingly. Have a little compassion. Think of the daily grind that appals and yet addicts them. Think of the gruesome beauty of their Consensus Model.

Han van der Horst is a historian and the author of *The Low Sky: Understanding the Dutch*.

THE DUTCH MODEL (2)

For the past six years, the 'Dutch model' has led to a situation in which the national government is formed by a coalition of political opposites, parties that were sworn enemies in the past. The red of the Socialists and the blue of the Liberals have mingled to form a coalition known as 'Purple'. The Cabinet governs a country where debate, unlike bureaucracy, seems to have been outlawed.

The political wing of the 'Polder Model'

Mark Kranenburg

In the Netherlands, spectacle and parliamentary debate do not go hand in hand. Sessions of the Second Chamber of Parliament are usually more akin to a library board meeting than to serious political discourse: very sound, never emotional. All of which fits in with the traditional Dutch saying: 'Just act normal, that's crazy enough.' As a result, the Parliament does not hold debates. Instead, it deliberates.

The best characterisation of Dutch parliamentary proceedings was once given by columnist H.J.A. Hofland: the apotheosis of polemic discourse is when one Member points to his chest and declares in an aggrieved tone to another Member that he never said such a thing.

Dutch politics is an oasis of calm, as it must be. Conflict is counter-productive. No single party has ever had anything even approaching an overall majority in parliament, so a coalition government is inevitable. This makes parties extremely cautious – today's enemy may be tomorrow's ally – especially at a time when the death of ideology has made it possible for almost all parties to work together.

For decades, the Christian Democrats played a pivotal role in the struggle for power. With the exception of the occupation years 1940-1945, they were represented in every government after the First World War. Sometimes they formed coalitions with the Social Democrats, sometimes with the Liberals. The Christian Democrats called the shots, the rest followed at a polite distance. The result was predictably consistent government policy.

This period of uninterrupted Christian Democrat rule came to an abrupt end in 1994, when the Liberals joined forces with the Social Democrats and condemned the Christian Democrats to the opposition benches. This coming together of supposedly irreconcilable extremes defied all prevailing coalition theories. The combination of Liberal 'blue' with Social Democratic 'red' prompted the name by which the coalition had been known since 1994: Purple (*Paars*). In fact, the two former adversaries got along so well that the coalition was prolonged after the 1998 general elections.

These smooth party relations may explain why things suddenly went awry in May 1999: calm seas can encourage carelessness. All of a sudden, the government tendered its resignation. Not because of fundamental policy disagreements, but because one awkward Senator from one of the coalition parties had managed single-handedly to block a bill to introduce a general referendum. This was the very piece of legislation that had been the decisive reason for D66, the smallest party in the coalition, to join the government in 1994. D66 was upset, blew the government to pieces, reflected on its position, and then settled for a compromise arrangement that allowed the government to be up and running again within three weeks. It allowed everyone to chant in unison that the purple coalition had emerged stronger from its ordeal.

The coalition between labour and capital that has governed the Netherlands since 1994 is best described as 'the Third *Way avant la lettre*', and a most successful way at that. The former trade union boss Wim Kok is now a Prime Minister worshipped by the business community. Big business was clear in its desire for a prolongation of the coalition under Kok's leadership after the last elections held in 1998. For business people, Kok's policy is the ideal combination of social planning combined with market incentives. Purple politicians refer to this as a sensible mix. At a gathering in Washington at the end of April 1999 to discuss the Third Way phenomenon, US President Bill Clinton said of Kok, 'he was doing it all before we were'.

Clinton's statement gives Kok more credit than he deserves. He may well be an exponent of the Third Way, but the mentality that underlines it is deeply rooted in Dutch culture. Some historians ascribe this to the geographical position of the Netherlands: without compromise and consensus, it would have been impossible for the Dutch to live together on a strip of land that is largely below sea level. It is not without reason that the Water Boards and their polder-pumping installations are the eldest tiers of government in the country. In his book *Hollands welbehagen* (The Well-being of Holland), Herman Pleij, Professor of Literature, writes: 'The Netherlands owes its existence to the democracy of dry feet. We need each other literally in order not to drown, and must subsequently rely on other countries for the means to stay alive.'

Our country relies on consultation, on the involvement in

REWARDS TO COMBAT SENSELESS VIOLENCE

ZWOLLE. **The province of Overijssel wants to introduce rewards of between 1000 and 5000 guilders for citizens who act sensibly to prevent or stop senseless violence. It is the first measure of its kind, and is intended to reward those working towards a safer community. Those who act to stop vandalism are also eligible.**

decision-making of as many people as possible. Although many people did not see it, the safety net of consensus has always remained in place, even during the wild 60s and 70s. Outside, on the barricades, rough language prevailed; but indoors, away from the public eye, compromises were being sought. Despite the rhetoric of struggle that was dished out to the grassroots, the avenues of communication always remained open.

Consensus has been institutionalised in the Netherlands, where the national identity is reflected in countless advisory and consultative bodies. Every issue bearing even the remotest risk of disagreement has a forum of its own in which all interested parties are represented, whether it be traffic issues, defence matters or education affairs.

Naturally enough, this culture of consultation has repercussions for politics. The more the relevant bodies agree, the less freedom of movement remains for the politicians. It was under these conditions that the now well-known 'Polder Model' was born in the early 80s. There were political plans to intervene in the country's wage levels: the government hoped to tackle the high rate of unemployment by sharply reducing labour costs. Facing the loss of their freedom of negotiation, unions and employers' organisations agreed to a voluntary wage restraint in return for a reduction in working hours. The political establishment had no choice but to acquiesce to this 'voluntary' agreement between employers and unions. It is no coincidence that, in the Netherlands, these two groups are referred to as the 'social partners'.

This trade-off of interests still lies at the heart of current socio-economic policy. The purple coalition is little more than the political wing of the Polder Model: a trade-off between the interests of the social democrats on the one hand and the liberals on the other. The decisions made are not so much principled choices as mathematical solutions. Everything that can be shared is shared. The Left gets its way in reducing defence spending, while the Right receives compensation in the form of a commensurate reduction in spending on overseas aid.

The success of the purple coalition allowed the political centre to govern the country without the need for the centrist party par excellence – the Christian Democrats. So far, things have gone smoothly – thanks in part to consistently good economic indicators. The distribution of available financial means remains the major component of national politics in the Netherlands. Continuing economic growth has removed the need for painful decisions.

As the co-operation between the Liberals and the Social-Democrats continues, the classic Left-Right divide recedes into the background, making way for a new divide between the material and non-material. Whether this will influence Dutch politics in the future remains to be seen. The essential strength of the system remains consensus: consultation will continue.

Politicians may change, but policy will remain familiar. If that is boring, so be it. European Commissioner Frits Bolkestein, former leader of the liberals and one of the most talked-about politicians of the last decade, once remarked that the more boring a country's politics, the happier its people. In the Netherlands, that would still seem to be the case.

Mark Kranenburg is a political commentator at NRC *Handelsblad*.

You need a what?

Danielle Pinedo

Mr P. taps impatiently on his formica tabletop. 'You haven't brought the document?'

'What document?' we ask in unison.

'The declaration of impediment. You need it for the marriage licence. I can't give you a marriage licence without it, and you can't get married without a licence.'

My fiancé and I come crashing down from cloud nine. Is this little bureaucrat serious? Can he really obstruct our marriage? I cough emphatically and look Mr P. straight in the eyes.

'You're not serious, are you?'

'I certainly am.'

'But how can we get this document within twenty-four hours? Hire a private jet?'

Earlier that morning, everything had seemed to be going smoothly. My fiancé was jealously guarding the pile of documents that the council had requested. Initially, Mr P. had seemed a helpful forty-something, but he had grown serious at the first sign of an irregularity from his computer. Had one of us lived abroad? Yes, I replied, as a student in Ohio. Had I been married there, he wanted to know. I jokingly replied that I hadn't had the time, considering my busy diary. As it turned out, however, Mr P. was not in the mood for jokes.

He thrust the telephone number for the Dutch consulate

in Cleveland into my hands. 'There will be a document on my desk by 4.30 p.m. tomorrow proving that you did not get married in Ohio.'

'Or else?'

'There will be no wedding.'

'But what about the time difference?' countered my fiancé. 'At 4.30 p.m. our time, they'll be having breakfast.' But Mr P. was already beckoning the next couple, number 905, to his desk.

Our race against the clock had begun. As it turned out, the number for the consulate was wrong. According to the lady at directory enquiries, there was no Dutch consulate in Cleveland. Aggrieved, I called Mr P., only to be informed that he was in a meeting, 'indefinitely'. So I decided to ring the town hall in Mount Vernon, Ohio, the same one that had once given me my social security number.

When I got through to Gale in Mount Vernon, she was

PARLIAMENT SUPPORTS SUNDAY REST BILL

THE HAGUE, 5 JULY. **A Bill introduced by the Labour Party (PvdA) and the Christian Union to give employees the right to refuse to work on Sundays has drawn support from a large majority in the Second Chamber of Parliament. Only the Liberal Party (VVD) opposes the measure, describing it as 'superfluous' and 'damaging to employers.' The Bill is intended to reconfirm Sunday as a collective day of rest. The proposed legislation will also enable workers to refuse to work irregular hours.**

willing to help, but unable to hide her surprise. 'You need a what?' When I explained the situation, she roared with laughter. 'What kind of a requirement is that? It's like having to prove that you're alive.' I giggled along with her, but my panic was mounting.

The spokesman at the American Embassy in The Hague wasn't able to help either. He 'was aware of the problem' and had been asked the question 'before'. He considered the requirement (one maintained only in the Netherlands) 'ridiculous'. There was, however, nothing he could do for me, 'certainly not at such short notice'.

The next morning, Mr P. received a surprise visit from my fiancé. Was he, my fiancé asked, equally nasty to his friends? Why hadn't the council mentioned the required document in its correspondence? My fiancé demanded a solution. Mr P. flushed and grabbed his chair for support. An uncompromising silence ensued. Salvation came in the form of a gnarled civil servant in his fifties.

'P., why don't you go and have lunch? I'll handle this,' he said in a tone both conciliatory and admonishing. Mr P. slunk off, his pasty cheeks blushing with growing fury. The newcomer introduced himself as Mr Van V., and told my fiancé that there was only one alternative. 'Your girlfriend must declare under oath that she is not married.'

And so I did. I solemnly swore that I was not a bigamist. After the ceremony, Van V. leaned over the table with a conspiratorial look. 'We've discussed the matter with the committee. As from today, aspiring couples will be informed of the requirement by letter.' My fiancé jumped up and sneered mildly: 'Long live Dutch bureaucracy.'

Danielle Pinedo is an editor at NRC *Handelsblad.*

ARTS

The Dutch art climate is free and innovative. While past governments generally took a backseat approach, the current Minister of Culture has not shied away from public debate.

Hands-off policy for a thriving sector

Mark Duursma

A few years ago, at the Rotterdam Film Festival première of Karim Traïda's film *The Polish Bride*, I was seated next to a critic from the American magazine *Variety*. The thing that struck him most about this very Dutch film was the sheer ugliness of it all. The wallpaper! Were all our farms that ugly on the inside? And as for the two lead characters, what audacity to cast such unattractive actors!

A fresh perspective can produce some interesting observations. Doubly so in this case, because the Dutch critics were very enthusiastic about the Algerian-born film maker's loving portrayal of the Groningen countryside. An outsider sees the beauty that we no longer see. Of course, not everything an outsider sees is beautiful, as a famous dialogue from Quentin Tarantino's *Pulp Fiction* aptly demonstrates. Returning from a European trip, Gangster 1 tells Gangster 2 about the disgusting Dutch habit of eating french fries with mayonnaise, 'I seen 'em do it, man. They fuckin' drown 'em in that shit.'

In general, the Dutch make poor chauvinists, except when it comes to art. Whether it be a jazz musician landing a contract with a prestigious American record label or a documentary maker winning a prize at an obscure Japanese film festival, every Dutch artist who achieves foreign success fills me with pride. Art is, after all, the barometer of a nation: the more exciting the art, the more interesting the country. See

Switzerland. On this scale, the Netherlands does very well. Not because of the last century's great painters or the international allure of the Concertgebouw Orchestra and The Netherlands Dance Theatre. Not even because of the number of foreign languages into which the works of authors such as Cees Nooteboom and Harry Mulisch are being translated.

It is design, photography and architecture that rank current Dutch art amongst the best in the world. Benno Premsela, Anton Corbijn and Rem Koolhaas (the latter two still very much active) paved the way for today's twenty and thirty-somethings who share the same desire for renewal. There is always room at the Dutch Opera for exciting new guest producers, which has helped make it one of the most talked-about opera houses in the world. Although theatre is a much more difficult product to export, it is clear that the repertory theatre adaptations here are infinitely more progressive than those in neighbouring countries. Dutch art academies attract many foreign students, while at the same time many art institutions have foreign directors.

NEW CODE OF CONDUCT FOR POLITICIANS

THE HAGUE. **In a letter sent to Parliament this morning, Internal Affairs Minister De Vries announced new rules intended to allow closer public scrutiny of politicians' financial behaviour. His proposals include a legally enforceable code of conduct for local politicians, mayors, aldermen and council members, who will be subjected to rules on outside business interests and positions and how to deal with gifts from third parties.**

The current art climate in the Netherlands is free and innovative. The government makes sure that the facilities are in place, but otherwise takes a backseat approach to policy-making. Liberal doctrine has clearly caught on. The Ministry of Education, Culture and Science is even pulling out of the logistics of state subsidies, and instead channelling funds for some institutions and individuals into a number of distribution agencies for specific branches of the arts. In the past decade, the state museums have been made much more independent from the state.

In a system that is quite unique in the world, value judgements about cultural subsidies are left to an independent Arts Council. This Council consists of discipline-bound commissions with members from the arts field itself. The obvious advantage of this judgement-by-experts is inside knowledge of the subject matter; the disadvantage is a too-closed circuit: artists judging colleagues.

Until recently, politicians stayed out of the cultural debate, largely because the consensus was too great. There were differences of opinion on matters of sex and money, confirming the cliché view of the Netherlands as a country of vicars and merchants. Dutch-based Iranian writer Kader Abdolah once voiced his amazement at the excitement caused in a tolerant country such as this over the question of what forms of nudity were permissible in art. The 1999 Holland Festival drew extra publicity (and visitors) after the State Prosecutor's office confiscated nine photographs from the Attack! exhibit. A judge later ruled that the prosecutor had been wrong in deeming the images to be child pornography, and that was the end of the matter.

Money is the other reason for public excitement about the arts. In 1998, The Hague's Gemeentemuseum (Municipal Museum) bought *Victory Boogie Woogie*, Mondriaan's last work, from an American collector for eighty million guilders. The Dutch Central Bank provided the money for the purchase, as a gesture to Dutch society marking the disap-

pearance of the guilder and the introduction of the Euro.
The gesture was not appreciated: the letters pages of the
newspapers were filled for weeks with readers' suggestions of
better ways to spend eighty million guilders. Meanwhile,
Parliament was unhappy about the rather underhand financ-
ing construction. Central Bank chairman Wellink was forced
to apologise in a later interview. Next time, he said, the money would be given to single mothers; that coming from a
man who had obviously never been particularly enthusiastic
about the whole idea.

There is a very strong tradition in the Netherlands that
politicians refrain from value judgements about the arts. In
the 1980s, Culture Secretary Brinkman tried to stop the P.C.
Hooft Prize, a major literary award, from going to the con-
troversial writer Hugo Brandt Corstius. The affair is still
regarded as a low point in the art world's relations with government. The current minister, the Social-Democratic economist Van der Ploeg, is smart enough to avoid that pitfall.
Politicians are rarely interested in areas where everything is
going smoothly, so Van der Ploeg decided to all but hijack the
cultural debate.

Since his appointment in autumn 1998, he has made it clear
that he prefers a demand-side approach to arts policy. His

point is that too few people are actively involved in the subsidised arts, and that young people and those of foreign descent are being left out. He wants to reach out to a broader audience in two ways: firstly, by using new criteria ('social reach', 'subsidy per visitor') for the evaluation of subsidy applications; and secondly, by granting more attention and resources to cultural diversity and culture in the schools.

With some minor adaptations, Van der Ploeg got his plans through parliament. He has certainly provided the writers of editorials with employment for some time to come. While his supporters refer to the arrogance and laziness of the established culture, opponents accuse his department of confusing culture policy with social policy.

The major question for the future is whether the increasing emphasis on the demand side (the 'public reach') of the arts will eventually be to the detriment of the supply side (the quality of art being offered). For that is the only thing that everyone in the debate seems to agree on: there is nothing wrong with the quality of the arts in the Netherlands.

Mark Duursma is an art editor at NRC *Handelsblad*.

DAYTRIP

There is more to see in the Netherlands than clogs, tulips and windmills. Leave Amsterdam for a journey by train, boat and bus and enjoy changing landscapes, cities old and new, and a man-made nature reserve.

Travel through landscapes and through time: a day trip

H.J.A. Hofland

There are no sleeping compartments on domestic Dutch trains, and there are very few domestic flights. If you live in Den Burg, on the island of Texel, and need to attend a morning meeting in Maastricht, an overnight stay is unavoidable. If you need to go to a birthday bash in Sluis in the province of Zeeland-Flanders, but happen to be on Schiermonnikoog, you'll need to bring a toothbrush. Almost every other return journey within the Netherlands can be made in a single day. Dutch literature has nothing to equal Paustovsky, Chekhov, Jack London or Jack Kerouac. However broad the horizon, it always contains a few houses. It is, in short, a small country.

Nevertheless, it is possible to make great journeys in the Netherlands, combining beautiful, flowing landscapes with visits to unique sights. I could advise you to take a train via Zutphen, the town of the many towers, to Kampen and to visit the largest cigar on earth (according to the Guinness Book of Records). Or perhaps a visit to Delfzijl, in the far north-east of the country, to visit the park with the statue of Maigret, that immortal creation of Georges Simenon, who chose the port town as the setting for one of his books.

Instead, however, let me suggest the following itinerary. Why this route? Because it condenses the entire country into less than twelve hours. It will take you – by train, boat and bus – through the centuries, from 1540 to the present day, past glories past, forgotten and new, through magnificent landscapes and over the water until the land itself disappears. Start at Amsterdam Central Station, and buy a train ticket to Lelystad.

Take the 7.10 train. Amsterdam Central Station! The heart of the country! When the station was built in 1895, Lelystad hadn't even been dreamt of. On its present site flowed a vast expanse of water, the Zuiderzee. Those wanting to cross it had two options: take the train around, or take the night boat across to Lemmer in Friesland.

The night boat left from the quay behind the station. Relatives would wave as the ship departed into the autumn night, slowly disappearing into the mist. Perhaps a storm would brew up. On the river IJ, the water might still be calm, but on the Outer IJ the seas would be getting choppy. As the moon broke through the clouds and cast its light on the blue-black mass of water below, the white crests would swell and disappear like the heads of shipwrecked passengers who will never return to shore.

Throughout the centuries, thousands of ships were lost on the Zuiderzee. The wrecks are strewn across the seabed, which is now a polder. When excavated, they are a treasure-trove for archaeologists. Allied planes downed over the water during the war are occasionally found as well. Sometimes the crew was unable to extricate itself; the remains are carefully recovered, relatives in Britain, America or wherever are traced, and the bodies are sent home for burial with the honours they deserve, fifty years after the fact.

The 7.10 train to Lelystad is a double-decker. Second class is almost as comfortable as first class. It doesn't matter whether you sit on the right or the left, but the view is better from the upper deck. At first you don't really notice that you are leaving Amsterdam behind, because the city – like all modern ones – extends through endless housing estates, modern offices and factories. Little by little, the cities are eating away at the meadows. That is very obvious here. Between Amsterdam and Weesp we see the Netherlands' biggest problem: the struggle for the distribution of land.

Every square foot is fought over by city planners and spokesmen, and by the ecologists, defenders of the ancient countryside. The party of economic expansion has been winning for years, and the country has become richer and uglier as a result. In the national fight for space, the urban agglomeration in the western provinces is the daily front line.

We are twelve minutes into our journey; it is 7.22. Change trains at Weesp; the 7.24 service to Lelystad leaves from the other side of the platform. Now watch carefully. The train travels a few more miles over the old land that has been here for centuries, before going over a bridge.

We are now surrounded by water: the IJmeer to the left, the Gooimeer to your right. After that, we're on new land, southern Flevoland to be precise. Here, thirty years ago, the seabed became visible after seven months of pumping water. Very little land on our planet is as new as that of southern Flevoland.

At 7.33 the train stops in Almere, a city of more than 100,000 inhabitants. It is the youngest of the Netherlands' boom towns, in an area which retains a 'frontier' atmosphere. The first pioneers, a few dozen, began building here in 1976. Ten years later, the 50,000th inhabitant was registered, with the 100,000th following some eight years after that. While the city continues to grow, our journey pushes inexorably on, into the new country, to Lelystad.

The city is named after the engineer C. Lely, who came up with the idea of draining the Zuiderzee over a hundred years ago. Many competing plans were made, but it was Lely's plan which was (largely) carried out in the long run. Our train continues across virgin lands, fertile soil for grain, fruit, cattle and all manner of useful things. Soon, however, we reach a different landscape, marshy, full of shrubbery and trees which are not arranged in straight lines but which grow and die according to where the seeds fall. These are the Oostvaarders Plassen, a wild, unfettered and totally man-made nature reserve.

In this perfectly proportioned countryside, even freedom comes in pre-fabricated form. A bird of prey drops out of the sky to catch a rat, but that is allowed here. In fact, the idea is for as many birds of prey to catch as many small, helpless rodents as possible. In the Dutch countryside, that is how things go.

The Dutch enjoy this. Seeing something like this makes us feel a little wild ourselves. But not for long, because the train reaches Lelystad at 7.55. This remarkable settlement is nine years older than Almere, but has remained smaller. We'd like to have a look around here, but we simply haven't much time. Remember, we have to be back in Amsterdam within twelve hours. Bus 150 to Enkhuizen leaves from the front of the station at 8.32.

We now commence the strangest part of our journey. After a few minutes, it seems like the bus is about to drive straight into the sea. Never fear however, for we are merely starting a 35-kilometer journey over a dike. Water on both sides, so what's the dike for? To connect Lelystad to Enk-huizen. But is this an important trading route? No. As it turns out, this dike was built by mistake.

The project was completed in 1976, by which time many people had noticed that countryside was becoming an increasingly rare phenomenon in this country. Build another polder? At the expense of the wild water, the fish, the birds and the people who owned sailing boats? A re-think was called for. After ten years of hesitation, construction of the Markerwaard – as this polder was due to be named – was postponed and never again seriously considered.

But the dike is here! As a monument, complete with motorway. The cost per kilometre is probably among the highest in the Dutch road network. If the construction costs were included in the bus fare, a return from Schiphol to Kennedy Airport would probably be cheaper.

This magnificent and priceless part of our journey takes only 35 minutes, after which we arrive in Enkhuizen. It is 9.07, and it's almost impossible to believe that we left Amsterdam only two hours ago.

Enkhuizen is one of the most beautiful towns in the Netherlands. Fortunately, we have plenty of time, because our boat doesn't leave until 12.42. It's probably best to pop over to the tourist office for a brochure. There is a great deal on offer, for the town contains more Dutch history than I can recount in a single newspaper paragraph. There is one detail I should mention, however: the museum of ships in bottles. Three centuries ago, the ships for the East Indies left from Enkhuizen. The Dutch fleet ruled the oceans of the world. Enkhuizen still has its museum of bottled ships: they will never set sail again, but the memories live on.

Take the time for a leisurely walk along the docks, relax at one of the bars by the old tower, the Dromedary and then go back to the station. The track ends where the wide seas begin. The most beautiful train stations are those at quaysides, on the boundary of two worlds. The boat to Stavoren should already be moored up. Get a ticket, hop on board and, after the sound of the ship's whistle, the ferry will make its way out of the harbour. Halfway to our destination, at the point of no return, we can see nothing but water in all directions.

The journey takes about an hour and a half. We get off the boat at Stavoren, an old merchant town where the trading routes to France, England and Latvia used to start, and where no more than a thousand people live today. It is 14.07. The town is picturesque, its history is fascinating, but has a tragic ending. We have little time for sightseeing, however, because the diesel train to Leeuwarden, the Frisian capital, leaves at 14.14.

Our journey across the Frisian prairies takes more than three-quarters of an hour. Here and there, the large farms look like pyramids. A Frisian farmer is an emperor on his own land, and we can see why. We arrive in Leeuwarden at 15.07. If the trains are running on time, we have 29 minutes to wait for the InterCity service to Amsterdam, which arrives there at 17.59.

You might say that not much could happen on such a fast train. But remember: you're travelling through the country-side to which Vincent van Gogh moved on 11 September 1883, and where he made some of his most famous paintings: the land of the Potato Eaters. The farmers here used to live in turf huts. On 15 September 1883, Van Gogh wrote to his brother Theo: 'Just to give you an idea of how authentic this region is. While I was painting in the hut, two sheep and a goat came to graze on the roof of this residence. The goat climbed up to the ridge and looked down the chimney. The woman, hearing something on the roof, shot outside and flung her broom at the aforementioned goat, which, nimble as a chamois, jumped down.'

So look outside and think of Van Gogh and the aforementioned goat. After Zwolle, the bridge over the IJssel, the river which provides the IJsselmeer with water, comes into view. Then the Veluwe, where the first Dutchmen, the Batavians, dwelled. After Amersfoort, we finally return to the urban agglomeration in the West that we left in an eastwards direction this very morning. Around the world, the Dutch world, in less than twelve hours.

Hofland's Tour

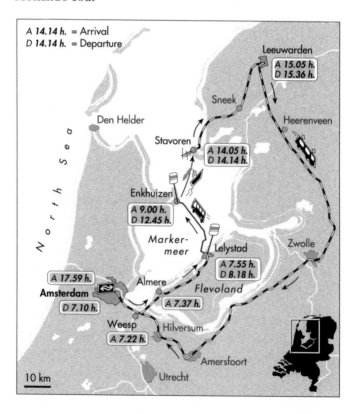

THE DUTCH MODEL (3)

In economic terms, the Netherlands is one of the most successful countries in Western Europe. Nevertheless, the 'Dutch Model' for managing social and economic relations is in need of a boost.

Not quite smart enough

Eduard Bomhoff

The Netherlands is becoming increasingly popular with international investors. The most recent *World Competitiveness Yearbook* places the country fourth out of the 47 countries investigated. On the specific point of 'internationalisation', the country is at second place, and in 'management' the score is also second from the top, with only the US rated more highly.

Such tables represent a combination of factual information about competitiveness, fiscal pressures and other easily measured statistics, compiled from the results of a detailed survey of more than 4000 managers. The results are in line with the impression of Dutch Treasury Minister Vermeend, who remarked a few years ago that the Netherlands figures prominently on most short-lists, when foreign investors evaluate the establishment in Europe of a distribution centre, a new office or head office or nowadays, even a factory. No country could win each and every contest for inward investment, but reaching so many final selection lists is a reassuring indication that the 'Dutch disease' has been overcome. A Taiwanese entrepreneur who sets up a bicycle factory outside Lelystad must assume that some things will go well in the polder!

Along with Ireland, Spain, and Finland, the Netherlands is currently one of the more successful countries in Western Europe. As is the case everywhere else, our present success is more temporary than we, in our present state of euphoria, would like to accept, and has more than one cause. Nevertheless, the Dutch comeback is remarkable, and is due mainly to three more or less concurrent factors in 1982 and 1983.

In November 1982, in the so-called Wassenaar Agreement, the trade unions agreed to end automatic wage indexation, in return for employers' commitment to place the subject of reducing working hours high on the agenda for collective labour contract negotiations. In March 1983, the Netherlands put a definitive end to monetary independence by pegging the level of the guilder to the German mark. In that same year, the first Lubbers government succeeded in convincing the Dutch people that benefits and civil servants' salaries had to be frozen for a number of years. This implied a decline in purchasing power, since there would be no compensation for inflation.

One result of the recession in which the Dutch economy found itself at the time was that Dutch employees were four times as likely to be made redundant as their German colleagues. It is thus hardly surprising that trade unions remained extremely cautious in their wage demands and employers remained unable to offer higher salaries until the end of the 1980s.

However, the exchange rate with the German mark no longer reacted to differences in cost levels between Germany and the Netherlands. As a result, Dutch products became progressively cheaper than German ones. Dutch and German companies use basically the same machines, and, given the fixed exchange rate, pay the same amount for imports of oil and other products. Every year, however, Dutch companies saw their labour costs decline in comparison with the German competition.

As a result, the Netherlands was able to develop a cost advantage of up to 15 percent over Germany in the course of the years 1983-1995. Over the last five years, Dutch wage increases have been slightly higher than in Germany, thereby nibbling at that advantage; at the current rate, however, wage costs in Holland will remain below the level in Germany for at least the next ten years.

Should we applaud the creativity of Chris van Veen, then chairman of the employers, and Wim Kok, then trade union leader and now Prime Minister, for abolishing wage indexation in the Wassenaar Agreement? Certainly, but we should also remember that these very same employers and trade unions had honestly believed, throughout the 1970s, that increasingly high wage increases would stimulate consumer spending and therefore be good for employment in the retail sector.

President Zijlstra of the Dutch Central Bank (De Nederlandsche Bank) warned repeatedly throughout the 1970s that inflation would damage the economy, and would not bring about a long-term reduction in unemployment. But his words fell on deaf ears. This was due not only to the ideological hang-ups of politicians in The Hague, but also to misunderstandings between employers and unions.

In other words, let us by all means praise the employers and unions for the Wassenaar Agreement and the period that followed, but at the same time let them share in the blame for the mistakes of the Seventies.

The success of the Dutch model, the so-called 'Polder Model', therefore represents little more than the Netherlands catching up with its neighbours. For many years, there were relatively few people at work in the Netherlands; we are now almost back at the European average. But now that we have finally caught up with the rest, mightn't it be time for us to do a little overtaking as well?

The Netherlands will never be Europe's sweatshop economy. We are far too attached to subsidised public transport, good-quality housing (even for those who cannot afford it), comprehensive insurance coverage against medical calamities, social security benefits that are higher than in the Anglo-Saxon countries and, finally, a serious contribution to overseas development aid.

If we're not going to be cheap, however, we have to be smart. It is unacceptable, for example, that so many immigrant pupils in our cities leave school for one or two years to return to their original home country, or even drop out altogether without qualifications.

International research clearly demonstrates that the average quality of education strongly influences the level that a country can attain. The public debate emphasises the importance of universities, mostly because these are staffed by university lecturers who like to publish articles on the editorial pages. Although good universities are obviously important, good primary and secondary education with low drop-out rates are even more important for economic growth.

Of the world's four transhipment economies – Hong Kong, Singapore, Belgium and the Netherlands – the former two have become almost as rich as the latter two, largely as a result of low taxation, favourable geographic location and good education.

Education is an important aspect of Chinese culture, as illustrated by the fact that a professor in Hong Kong earns up to twice as much as his colleague in the Netherlands, and by the high scores attained by East Asian pupils in international comparisons. If the Netherlands wants to stand out internationally, it will have to take education more seriously.

This requires a change in thinking at the Ministry of Education. The current minister is better than the devotee of central planning who occupied his post during the period 1989-'98. Yet so far he has not been able to strike the deal with the unions that is necessary to achieve a meaningful increase in the freedom of teachers and school principals to use the resources in the way that most benefits their pupils. The teachers' unions remain opposed to variable pay for teachers, and to all schemes that aim at rewarding schools that do a good job. Public opinion is keenly interested in better primary and secondary education but methods that have been successful abroad always involve more freedom for school managers; a taboo for the Dutch unions.

More money is required in primary and secondary education, preferably to be spent by the schools directly. Ministers and civil servants may claim that the extra money should be spent on reducing class sizes, but how do they know? A headmaster may feel that the money could be better spent on increasing the pay of the IT or maths teacher, on new computer equipment, or on strengthening management so as to better combat truancy and vandalism. Such decisions should be taken away from civil servants' desks and entrusted instead to the front-line school leadership.

Clearly, improvements in education will not immediately result in increased economic growth. But, in the long term, a country like the Netherlands (especially as natural gas reserves begin to dwindle) needs to excel first and foremost in the quality of its labour force. This requires, first of all, a flexible labour market – one in which people are properly rewarded and not made to pay more than half of their income in taxes, and in which the unemployed are quickly helped to get off benefits and back to work. On the other hand, it requires top-quality education, something in which the Netherlands has lagged behind over the last few years, probably as a result of an unfortunate combination of budget cuts and over-regulation.

For a few years, the Netherlands will remain significantly cheaper than Germany. That gives us time to use the propitious economic circumstances in which we find ourselves to tackle the sensitive issues that remain: these include rail privatisation, less Stalinist planning and more patient rights in the medical sector, larger houses for a more prosperous population and, finally, the mounting of a serious offensive on the traffic problem. This will provide the litmus test for the Dutch model.

The excellent economic figures of the last few years represent a correction of the equally serious mistakes made in the past by both employers and unions. If, however, our culture of consensus also proves capable of energetically injecting more freedom and competition into our economy, I will gladly take off my professional hat to the Dutch model!

E.J. Bomhoff is director of the Nyfer Forum for Economic Research, and Professor of Economics at the Nijenrode University.

THE LANGUAGE

The Dutch language teems with English words and their derivatives. Less is known about the opposite: the many words in the English language borrowed from the Dutch. Some 21 million people in the Netherlands, Flanders and Surinam speak the Dutch language. Many people will be surprised to learn that the language is taught around the world at more than 250 universities in 48 countries, from Poland to China. More Germans study Dutch than vice versa. The Dutch tend to look down on their own language, but on a world-wide ranking of some 6000 languages, Dutch comes in 35th in a comparison of the number of speakers.

It is widely, and falsely, believed that the oldest known sentence in the Dutch language is 'Hebban olla vogala nestas hagunnan, hinase hic enda thu' ('All the birds have started building their nests, except you and me'). But this text, discovered in Oxford in 1932, dates from around 1100, while other fragments of Dutch texts have since been recovered dating back to the ninth and tenth centuries.

Latin charters have also given us the names of a handful of people, places, fields and rivers. The Dutch language is the product of a confluence of various dialects, in which the language of the province of Holland eventually gained the upper hand. The principal reason for this was the political predominance of Holland in the seventeenth century.

The 'States Translation' of the Bible, completed in 1636, also furthered linguistic unification. A strong difference has always remained, however, between written and spoken Dutch. Historians draw a distinction between Old Dutch, Middle Dutch and New Dutch.

Dutch has never been legally established as the formal language of the Netherlands, but Flanders did take precisely such a step on 10 December 1973. Over the last few years, discussion has centred around whether Flanders should adopt its own standard language, Standard Flemish. The Flemish Language Society recently drew up a distinct Flemish spelling. The most significant linguistic difference between Flanders and the Netherlands is that the Flemish are used to speaking a dialect alongside the standard language, whereas dialects are gradually disappearing from Dutch.

Waffles, booze and more loan words

Nicoline van der Sijs

Over the centuries, the Dutch language has loaned out a large number of words to foreign languages. Even in this century (the century during which Dutch has been, according to many pessimists, in increasing danger of becoming a dialect of English), Dutch words have found their way into other languages.

The word most recently adopted by a whole series of languages is *klapschaats*. During the last few years, this skate, developed at the Amsterdam's Free Protestant University, has given Dutch speed-skaters a technical advantage and considerable success. Other countries have adopted the invention and its name. During the world all-round speed-skating championships in Nagano, in early 1997, the Japanese spoke of *kurappusukaatsu* (there is no distinction between the sound of the l and r in Japanese), the Norwegians of *klapp-skøyte* and the Germans of *Klappschlittschuh*. The International Skating Union has afforded the *klapskate* (English) an official status.

And what about words lent out in the past? Which language has borrowed the greatest number of Dutch words? If we disregard the former Dutch colonies, the answer, ironically enough, is English. The *Oxford English Dictionary*, the treasury of the British English lexicon from the middle of the twelfth century to the present, lists about 1500 Dutch words and about 300 words from Afrikaans, the Dutch-derived language of the white South Africans.

The influence of Dutch on American English is much more modest: the four-volume *Dictionary of American English on Historical Principles* lists only about 150 words. Apart from this small group, a number of words are only found in isolated areas formerly inhabited by Dutch colonists. J. Bense's *Dictionary of the Low-Dutch Element in the English Vocabulary*, published in 1939, describes all the Dutch and Low-German words ever used in English in any variant. The list comes to some five thousand words.

So why has Dutch had such a sizeable influence on the English language? And when did this begin? The English language first began borrowing words from Dutch in the twelfth century, a period when there were already trade contacts between the two language areas. Of the words borrowed during this period, the most common is dam.

More important, however, was the fact that William the Conqueror, Duke of Normandy, became King of England in 1066. Although William I himself spoke French, his entourage included a number of Flemish people, some of whom

---

HOSPITAL TO RECRUIT IN CINEMA

ROTTERDAM. **The IJsselland Hospital in Capelle aan de IJssel is trying to recruit anaesthetist assistants through advertising in cinemas. The hospital has been faced with unfilled vacancies for a number of months, and has had little success with ads in newspapers and professional magazines. The ad, entitled 'Is there an anaesthetist's assistant in the audience tonight?' will be shown for a month.**

subsequently settled in England. Between the Norman Conquest and the beginning of the eighteenth century, a steady stream of craftsmen emigrated to Great Britain from the Northern and Southern Netherlands. In industrial terms, they were superior to their English counterparts and were able to earn a comfortable living in England. They introduced novel forms of industry, of which weaving was to be the most important. This period therefore witnessed the introduction into the English language of loan words such as spool (*spoel*) and flock (*vlok*). Beer brewers introduced hop (*hop*), coop (*kuip*) and tub (*tobbe*). The English also adopted words for instruments, such as drivel (*drevel*), hack (*hak*), peg (*peg*), plug (*plug*) and tackle (*takel*).

During the sixteenth and seventeenth centuries, contacts between Great Britain and the Netherlands intensified, partly because of the large number of people fleeing from the Northern and Southern Netherlands to Great Britain during the Eighty Years War against the Spanish (1568-1648). Predictably enough, these two centuries witnessed the most concentrated linguistic interaction. Surprisingly, however, many of the words borrowed from Dutch in this period are not related to a specific field or trade. A large number of 'general' words were also adopted, including to bluff (*bluffen*), to booze (*buizen*), luck (*geluk*), to loiter (*leuteren*), to mangle (*mangelen*), pack (*pak*), to slip (*slippen*) and to smuggle (*smokkelen*).

From the eighteenth century on, the influence came less from the Netherlands than from South Africa, which the English took over from the Dutch at the end of the eighteenth century. This change of ownership had led the Boers (from the word *boeren*, meaning 'farmers') to begin on their Grote Trek (*trek*, 'trekking' in English), which temporarily took them beyond English jurisdiction. Although the English eventually conquered the area, Afrikaans did stage a linguistic fight-back: in the nineteenth and twentieth centuries, the number of words borrowed by the English from Afrikaans was significantly larger than the number borrowed directly from Dutch. The flora, fauna and landscape of South Africa proved to be a particular inspiration for the English language, yielding words such as *aardvark*, *aasvogel*, *hart(e)-beest*, *kloof*, *kraal*, *springbok*, *steenbok* and *wildebeest*. The infamous word 'apartheid' also found its way into English, and other languages, in this fashion, as did the loan translation 'homeland' for *thuisland*.

Dutch colonists made their way to America from the seventeenth century onwards. Inevitably, they took their food and customs with them, thereby providing the American language with a number of new words and items, such as bedspread (*beddensprei*), coleslaw (*koolsla*), cookie (*koekje*), Santa Claus (*Sinterklaas*), to snoop (*snoepen*), spook (*spook*), stoop (*stoep*) and waffle (*wafel*).

Twentieth-century Dutch influences on the English language have mostly been restricted to science. The English words 'superconductor' and 'superconducting' are translations of *supergeleider* and *supergeleidend*, terms coined by Heike Kamerlingh Onnes, who discovered superconduction in 1911 and received the Nobel Prize for it in 1913. Other Dutch scientists were able to attach their names to inventions and thereby become part of the English language. If a discovery was important, foreign scientists were prepared to hurdle the language barrier in the bargain. This is illustrated by a remark made by the Scottish physicist James Clerk Maxwell, to the effect that Van der Waal's 1873 dissertation had led more than one researcher to learn Dutch. Other examples of phenomena named after Dutch scientists include Van der Waals' forces, the Zeeman effect, the Casimir effect, Lorentz contraction, Van 't Hoff's equation, Oort('s) (comet) cloud, the Kuiper belt and the Vroman effect.

The Dutch language resembles other languages, in that it currently borrows many words from English. Considering the sheer number of words being borrowed, one would expect some of these supposedly 'English' words to actually be of Dutch origin. These words return to the mother tongue, albeit with an often new, specifically English meaning and form. The majority of these words are international: they are borrowed from English by many different languages. As a result, it is through English that Dutch words are still able to spread throughout the linguistic world.

Nicoline van der Sijs is an etymologist.

LOAN WORDS

English words originally loaned from the Dutch and now loaned back:

boss	baas
brandy[1]	brandewijn
cruiser	kruiser
dope	doop, 'doopsaus'[2]
gin[3]	jenever
golf	kolf
pickles	pekel
rack	rek
scoop[4]	schop
shock	schok
skate	schaats
sketch	schets
skipper	schipper
snack	snakken, 'happen'
yacht	jacht
yawl	jol

1 older form: brandewine

2 This word has taken a new meaning in English.

3 older form: geneva

4 In American English, this word has taken on a new meaning, shifting from 'clipping' or 'excerpt' to 'exclusive news'.

PAINTING

Seventeenth-century Dutch painting left clear marks on the English language:

easel	ezel
(to) etch	etsen
foreground	voorgrond
(to) enlist	inlijsten
landscape[1]	landschap
masterpiece	meesterstuk
still life	stilleven
stipple	stippel

[1] The second part of the word 'landscape' has been detached in the English and acquired a distinct meaning: panorama, view. This is used to make new words, such as cityscape, cloudscape, moonscape, seascape and, most recently, the internet software company Netscape.

WARFARE

Many Dutch military terms found their way into the English language in the course of the wars against the Spanish in the sixteenth century, and the Anglo-Dutch Wars of the seventeenth century:

beleaguer	belegeren
furlough	verlof
hireling	huurling
knapsack	knapzak
lifeguard	lijfgarde
onslaught	aanslag
plunder	plunderen
tattoo	taptoe
undermine	ondermijnen
uproar	oproer

Many English shipping terms are derived from Dutch:

deck	dek
dock	dok
iceberg	ijsberg
flyboat	vlieboot
freight	vracht
keelhaul	kielhalen
(to) laveer	laveren
maelstrom	maalstroom
nock	nok
reef	reef
scout	schuit
sheet anchor	schootanker
sloop	sloep

Dutch words: acid, airbag, babyfaced, bacon

Ewoud Sanders

Is Dutch still Dutch? As the following bit dialogue demonstrates, English words are increasingly forcing their way into the Dutch language.

'What language do they speak in the Netherlands?'

'Silly question: Dutch.'

'Well, that's what I thought, but I wasn't quite sure. Listen to the commercials on Dutch TV. At least half of them are in English. The same goes for shop fronts, road signs and billboards. You read and hear English and American everywhere.'

'It's like that all over the world.'

'Sure, but it's even worse in Holland.'

'Aren't you exaggerating a little?'

'No, not at all. When my three-year-old cousin is enthusiastic about something, he shouts: "Yes!" When he's angry, it's: "Shit!" His elder sister says: "Fuck!" It's the same all over the country, and they all seem to think it's perfectly normal.'

'Well, it had struck me that everyone says "okay" all the time.'

'Lots of countries do that. The word "okay" is America's most successful export product.'

'But do the Dutch really consider it normal, all that English?'

'Not entirely. There seem to be two groups. Some people say: "What's the problem? Every language borrows from other languages; English just happens to be the dominant language at the moment. A lot of English words are 'Dutchi-fied', and others are quickly replaced, so there isn't really a problem." Other people actively resist the English influence. One magazine campaigns for Dutch equivalents to be thought up for the English words that are creeping into the language. There's even a group called "Anglowaan" (Anglo-delusion) that's trying to save people from the delusion that English is somehow better than Dutch.'

'What do the Dutch writers do?'

'Some of them just ignore it completely, while others, in-cluding one of the most famous Dutch authors, predict that Dutch will be dead within fifty years. He stirred up quite a controversy when he said that, because his main reason for saying so was that his daughter always said "Shit!" when she hurt herself. That was his proof that Dutch would give up the ghost within half a century.'

'You can't be serious! What's the government doing about it?'

'A while ago, one minister said that English should be the

DOUBLE-INCOME COUPLES DRIVE UP HOUSING PRICES

ROTTERDAM. The growing number of dou-ble-income couples is causing house prices to rise. High living costs are, it seems, the driv-ing force behind emancipation. In 1975, the average home cost 140,000 guilders and was financed on a single income in 55 percent of cases. That price has now gone up to around 350,000 guilders, with only 25 percent of pur-chases financed with one salary.

main language at universities. While quiet efforts continue behind the scenes to strengthen the position of Dutch within the European Union, the government hasn't really taken part in the debate at all. In fact, the official list of Dutch words, which is compulsory for the education system and the civil service, is chock-full of English words. Look at it. Under A you find words like aboriginal, accountancy, ace, acid, act, aerobic, afrolook, aftershave, à go-go, aids, airbag, airconditioning, all in, all right, all risk, all-round, anchorman and appetizer. As for B, there's babyboom, babybox, babydoll, babyface, babysit, babysitter, backgammon, background, backhand, back-up, bacon… Need I continue?'

'No, no, that'll do. And these are words for which the Dutch government prescribes an official spelling?'

'Yes, you might say that these words are officially considered Dutch. Even the word 'shit' is in there, somewhere between shirtsponsor and shock.'

'No shit!'

'No, really!'

'All right, now I understand why you were wondering which language they speak here.'

Ewoud Sanders is a philologist and journalist.

DUTCH WORDS

batch, battledress, bazooka, beatgeneration, beauty, benefit of the doubt, black power, blow-out, board, bobtail, bock, body-art, bodyguard, bodyliner, bodyshaping, bodystocking, boobytrap, brainbox, braindrain, braintrust, brainwashing, breakdown, break-evenpoint, briefing, browning, buddyseat, bug, business, butterfly,

caddie, cakewalk, camcorder, candybar, cashflow, casting, centerfold, charter, checklist, cheerio, citybag, claim, clan, clean, clearing, closereading, coaster, cocktailshaker, coming man, counseling, counselor, country, covergirl, crackdealer, crazy, creamcracker, cross, cross-over, cruise, cue, cutter,

et cetera.

Source: *Woordenlijst Nederlandse taal*

SPORTS

For a country its size, the Netherlands has achieved con-siderable sporting success. Football in particular is very popular; it has the power to transform the Netherlands into an 'orange' country. And everyone skates in Holland. Ever heard of the Elfstedentocht?

Less orange in uneven years

Jaap Bloembergen

Holland is a country of green pastures and drab grey housing estates. But every other year, during the winter and summer months, half the country goes dressed in orange. During the international skating and football championships, as on the Queen's official birthday, the country has a carnival look to it.

During the European and World Championships, chauvinism knows no bounds in a country otherwise noted for its sobriety. Police officers decorate their uniforms and office workers at their terminals wear orange ties. With any luck, Crown Prince Willem-Alexander will be leading a polonaise somewhere: the House of Orange as the symbol of a nation's hopes.

There is a famous Dutch saying that goes: 'How a small country can still be great.' Gold medals go a long way in making up for a chronic lack of political and economic clout. And for a country its size, the Netherlands has achieved considerable sporting success. The fact that people outside the country are not particularly interested in speed-skating is of strictly secondary importance. Double Olympic medallist Gianni Romme is an international sports celebrity, at least in his own country.

Everyone skates in Holland, where an excess of water and a lack of snow combine to make for ideal skating conditions during the winter freeze. Where else can you find hundreds of thousands of people on the ice during severe winters? Pea soup is the staple diet of skaters who ride long-distance treks past windmills and dikes. Skating is a long-established tradition in Holland. Even in old paintings by masters such as Avercamp, there is always a skater gliding through some corner of the frame. Skating has a strong folkloric aspect to it.

Spectators at the major championships are usually less interested in the lap times that determine the outcome than in drinking beer and Beerenburger, a herbal spirit distilled in the northern province of Friesland. They sing themselves hoarse, their faces painted orange. At the same time, millions of people cluster around their televisions in defiance of the old American adage that watching skating is about as interesting as watching the grass grow.

The ultimate in skating pleasure, however, is the Elfstedentocht (Eleven Cities Tour), a race over two hundred kilometres, and past eleven Frisian cities. The tour can only be held during very severe winters, when the lakes and canals are frozen hard enough to bear the weight of so many skaters... and to allow water traffic to be suspended for an extended period of time. On the day of the Elfstedentocht, the Dutch economy grinds to a halt. The Crown Prince took part in the race anonymously in 1986.

Along with the paintings of Rembrandt and Van Gogh, football is an important aspect of Dutch culture. Between 1987 and 1994, when Marco van Basten was at the height of his divinity at AC Milan, the number of Italian tourists in the Netherlands rose by three hundred percent, all of them wanting a peek at the house where the great man had been born. Dutch holidays-makers in Greece between 1965 and 1985 were invariably treated to taxi drivers' appraisals of Johan Cruijff's talents. As the ambassador of a nation proud of its football, he was present at the birth of the philosophy that became known as Total Football, later adopted around the world.

Every Sunday evening between seven and eight o'clock, millions of people, most of them men, watch the highlights of the Dutch football league. As most of the top players have departed to richer clubs abroad, the standard of play in the domestic competition has plummeted over the last few years. Nevertheless, many families still eat their Sunday dinner in front of the television.

Ajax and Feyenoord have traditionally been the top clubs in Dutch football: each reflects the character of its support-ers. Ajax is a club schooled in technical ability, and is support-ed by the artists and horse-traders of Amsterdam. First and foremost, Feyenoord players are physically strong, drawing their most dedicated support from the Rotterdam dock workers. PSV Eindhoven does a reasonable job as an outsider. For years, PSV, lead by managers from the Eindhoven-based electronics giant, Philips, epitomised capitalism in sport. Today the increasing commercialisation of football has erod-ed the uniqueness of PSV's approach.

The Netherlands is much less orange in 'uneven' years, during which no European or World Championships, or Olympic Games, are held. Annual sporting events such as Wimbledon or the Tour de France appeal much less to the

---

SURROGATE MOTHER ESCAPES PROSECUTION

ROTTERDAM. The government prosecution service will not press charges against a paid surrogate mother. According to a gay couple from Hornhuizen, the woman gave birth to twins on their behalf in 1998, but has refused to give them up. A preliminary criminal inves-tigation carried out by public attorneys in Groningen found no evidence of any criminal wrongdoing.

popular imagination. Most people have no qualms about going on holiday during these summers and missing Richard Krajicek's exploits at Wimbledon or those of Michael Boogerd, Krajicek's primary school classmate, in the Tour de France.

Cycling is only really popular in the Catholic south of the Netherlands. After the Tour de France, the cyclists earn a great deal of money 'riding circles around the church', as these races are often called. If you look around the countryside these days, you will see that most cycling amateurs are middle-aged. The young have all but abandoned cycling, considering it a sport for mad endurance freaks.

Dutch athletes excel at outdoor sports, with the exception of indoor speed-skating. Despite the fact that the rainy climate might be seen to encourage the pursuit of indoor sports, international success in these disciplines is extremely rare. The major exception has been the men's volleyball team, which won gold at the 1996 Olympics. Since then, however, the team's form has deteriorated. Handball and basketball are in even more dire condition. The average Dutchman is only really interested in the NBA playoffs, which receive wide television coverage.

Korfball and field hockey have a distinct status in the Netherlands. Korfball is a poor excuse for basketball, with a wicker basket as a goal, instead of a net. It is a mixed-team sport that only the Dutch and the Belgians take seriously. Fanatic missionaries of korfball travel the world with balls and baskets in a brave attempt to convert the masses. This form of evangelism seems doomed to fail: korfball remains a sport for the Low Countries alone.

At least ten countries world-wide take field hockey seriously; of these, the Netherlands has the highest number of artificial-turf fields. The national teams are exceptionally good, with the men's team being the current holders of the World and Olympic titles, and the women's team perpetual runners-up to the Australians. Unlike in the United States, hockey in the Netherlands is not just a girls' sport. It is equally suited to macho men who have no difficulty downing a barrel of beer after a match. Membership of a hockey club is first and foremost a ticket to 'gezelligheid', a typically Dutch concept, the meaning of which is only partly conveyed in English by words such as companionship or conviviality.

Traditional pursuits such as gymnastics and athletics receive relatively little attention in the Netherlands. Physical education is relatively unimportant in Dutch schools, especially in comparison with countries such as Germany and the United Kingdom.

Added to this is the fact that the Dutch mentality is relatively unsuited to individual sports, displaying instead a marked preference for shared endeavour. The exceptional athletes who are prepared to train on their own for eight hours a day receive pitifully little support from the sports authorities or the government. It must be said, however, that matters have improved somewhat over the last few years. The international success of the swimming team is the logical consequence of a much more deliberate policy towards professional sport.

Jaap Bloembergen is a sports editor at NRC *Handelsblad*.

THE DUTCH MODEL (4)

The core of the Dutch model is described by the untranslatable word: 'gedogen'.

In essence, it means to consciously allow that which is officially prohibited. Out of pragmatism. That is the reason why soft drugs are prohibited in the Netherlands, while their use is permitted.

Conformist nonchalance

THE DUTCH WAY OF MANAGING THE UNMANAGEABLE

Marc Chavannes

The Netherlands is too small. This has a number of known practical disadvantages, but also one advantage: no one really cares what the Dutch get up to. As long as it doesn't create any problems requiring Richard Holbrooke's immediate attention, the world turns a blind eye. On occasion, a neighbouring President may even hope to boost his own image when the Netherlands once again experiments gently with life and living.

For that, clearly, is the result of the Netherlands' chronic lack of international newsworthiness: only those facts that seem to confirm an existing prejudice have any chance of making the foreign media. The stereotype in question is the Netherlands' seemingly casual tolerance of experiments with the trio of drugs, abortion and euthanasia. What the Netherlands does in these cases, to the dismay of many, is 'gedogen'. It is no coincidence that this word is untranslatable. What it really comes down to is that the Dutch consciously allow what is officially prohibited. The point being that these things are generally prohibited elsewhere as well, but happen there regardless, and in an unsupervised way.

A quick search of the World Wide Web allows us to refine the image of the Netherlands as the Mecca of 'gedogen'. Abortion is clearly less of an issue than it was in the seventies and eighties. In any case, the Netherlands no longer leads the way. UN statistics show that the Netherlands has the lowest abortion rate of a number of industrialised states: 98.5 per 1000 pregnancies, compared to 214.6 in France, 225.1 in the UK and 337.9 in the US.

In the American web-universe, the search phrase 'gedogen' takes us to the Seattle Times and 'The slippery slope in a flat land of tulips'. It refers to 'Holland, the acknowledged world leader in euthanasia'. It claims that 'in 1995 more than 50 percent of all patients who died while under medical care were hastened to their death by their doctor'. And even worse, 'in 62 percent of cases, this was done without the patient's consent or knowledge'. To drive the message home, the paper writes: 'This is the real-world laboratory where physician-assisted suicide has become routine and anything but rare'. Shock, horror – and no hint of further investigation. A distant cliché is safer than a more refined truth closer to home.

For a long time, French search engines responded to the word 'gedogen' by producing articles on Dutch drugs policy. The French correspondents in the Netherlands ably complemented their president's sound bites. The editorial and letters pages were particularly susceptible to radical simplifications of reality. Their solutions to the drugs problem generally depended on an absolute faith in prohibition, a logical translation of the French fascination with authority. In the last few years, however, the president has moderated his criticism. 'Gedogen' is still anathema, but as much – if not more – is 'overlooked' in France, which has significantly higher percentages of drug addicts and AIDS deaths than the Netherlands.

The French bulletin of old-style, left-wing political correctness, *Le Monde Diplomatique*, revels in abhorrence when it describes Dutch efforts to legalise and regulate voluntary commercial prostitution. 'Le corps humain mise sur le marché' (The human body put on the market) was its bloodcurdling headline. The integration of thoughts on sexual freedom and 'sexual labour' led the Dutch government to believe that prostitution, even in the long run, could not be done away with. The learned Parisian researcher shuddered to think that the Dutch government and parliament did not even entertain the illusion that abolition was the final goal.

On the question of tolerance, also when it comes to drugs policy, the British take an intermediate position. *The Economist* once made gleeful use of the word 'gedogen' to explain the twists and turns of Dutch policy. It has since emerged that research into medicinal uses for cannabis could only legally be carried out in Britain, albeit with seeds imported from the Netherlands, the world leader in cannabis production. The British had been pragmatic enough to license such research, whereas the Dutch authorities had grown cautious and refused.

Pragmatism has taken an ugly turn in Tony Blair's Britain, which is now trying to legalise the random interception of email traffic without any need for a preliminary search warrant. The UK secret services have a certain reputation for bungling their operations, so maybe this codification of an illegal reality will not harm organised crime too severely.

Then again, the English would never go so far as to design custom street furniture for the prostitution industry. In the Netherlands, these public permissiveness zones are unlikely to cause any great public outrage, if only because they have been given a practical, rather technical name: *afwerkplek*, another untranslatable term meaning something like 'fixing spot' or 'finishing room'. In fact, they even come in two shapes and sizes, depending on whether the customer has taken the car or the bicycle to come looking for lust.

Call it prudish or prudent, for the British this brand of realism is a bridge too far. While 'gedogen' in the Netherlands is simply a way of regulating public impotence, the British have taken their entire society to task. Not by organising more symbols, but by abolishing laws, civil servants and civilised means of public transportation. The all-powerful state has become a thing of the past, a fiction exploited for too many years: 'do-it-yourself' was the new creed. The newly elected Labour Party has seen no reason to disagree. The core of Thatcherite rhetoric turns out to have convinced more parties than the Conservatives alone. The socialist Education Secretary proudly announced how many businesses had invested in improving quality in education. Eighties right-wing slogans become nineties left-wing reality. Or is it simply the British way of keeping the unacceptable acceptable, in this case the poor quality of state education?

Each nation has its own need for self-respect. Over the centuries, rational strategies have been devised to keep the unmanageable pronounceable, formulas to maintain the fiction of law and order. The methods are no secret, but one can choose to ignore them. Those who exercise or seek to exercise power generally have a vested interest in pretending that everything is under control; pity, then, that the international media pay so little attention to the Netherlands.

One of the characteristics the would-be-virtuous Dutch admire most in themselves is their penchant for openness. They even leave their curtains open in the evening. There is no need for secrecy, not even in 'how we deal with dilemmas'. Wrestling with the drugs problem has become a national therapy session. 'Really tricky, drugs are banned by international treaties and therefore under Dutch law – but we don't believe in banning things that are going to happen anyway. We want to stop people switching from soft drugs to hard drugs. OK, so we'll just 'gedogen' the sale and personal use of soft drugs, but not the trade in them.'

Officials smile modestly. Critics prefer the word hypocrisy: no sale without trade. The leader of the Dutch Christian Democrats sees the same pattern in the approach to refugees and other would-be immigrants. He has said: 'The policy of not consistently deporting asylum seekers may seem humane, but is in fact the cruellest of all policies. The consequence, after all, is an illegal future, with no prospect of ever obtaining proper papers, a future in the margins of Dutch society.'

The national consensus, however, remains unperturbed. The Netherlands continues to welcome tens of thousands of migrants every year from all over the world, as it officially sticks to its drugs policy: 'Public health is more important than being macho and not solving anything. We don't live on an island, so we can't legalise soft drugs, let alone hard drugs. But then again, we don't appreciate the French and German politicians coming and lecturing to us every time they have an election year.'

The sociologist Hans Adriaansens put it differently. He wrote in the Utrecht University newsletter: 'Some countries are corrupt, others have a proper Mafia, the Netherlands has *gedogen*.' National sins come in all shapes and sizes, but it would be overly simplistic to see 'gedogen' as a typically Dutch national weakness, without putting the alternatives into perspective. The alternative to Mafia is no Mafia. The alternative to corruption is honesty. The alternative to 'gedogen' is to make tough and just laws, and see to it that they are strictly adhered to.

Almost no country on earth can manage that. The French Parliament has been struggling for years with an EU directive intended to preserve migratory birds and waterfowl. The purpose of the directive is to give the creatures a chance to breed, and so to make sure that there are enough to shoot next year. Millions of French hunters, ranging from very right-wing to very Communist in their political outlook, have indignantly flouted the directive. And the French Parliament, when it came to translating the European rules into national law, felt obliged to pass a clause that extended the hunting season by almost two months over and above EU law. The Greens were the only ones who voted against it. All other MPs gave in to the narrow-minded, nationalistic lobby of *Chasse, Pêche, Nature et Tradition*. After complaints from Brussels, the left-wing government was forced to come up with a new law – that has since been adopted – which less overtly contravened EU legislation.

After years of 'gedogen', France has resorted to legalising a practice that still is at odds with European law. According to Newsweek (22 June 1998): 'We don't think that France is a nightmare; we just think that it should be more like Holland.' If they really mean that, they have drastically underestimated European countries' need for territorially defined symbols of national identity. Following this American advice is the last thing France wants to do, for the simple reason that actual differences are becoming increasingly hard to find.

'*Gedogen* is delayed toughness, and therefore a politics of evasion and cowardice,' H.J.A. Hofland commented in the Dutch newspaper NRC *Handelsblad*. He was referring to the ongoing discussions about national airport Schiphol, currently the country's most important conflict zone. Schiphol is growing so rapidly that its noise pollution affects millions of people. Luckily for them, noise-pollution limits have become increasingly strict over the years. But then again, the Dutch can't afford to let their airport lose ground to competitors by refusing to let it grow. They don't want that, and a new policy of 'gedogen' is born.

Meanwhile, many of the areas in which the Netherlands have enjoyed an international reputation for tolerance have witnessed a backlash of one sort or another. Local residents have complained about prostitution often enough for local authorities in Amsterdam, Rotterdam and other cities to force it increasingly into narrowly defined zones of 'gedogen': small bits of no man's land where the authorities' deliberate tolerance is just about tolerated by the local population. People are increasingly militant about the negative impact of the drugs trade and casual street violence. Politicians talk about 'zero tolerance', then sit back, confident that they have adequately caught the public mood.

All the stories about Dutch tolerance must be taken with a grain of salt anyway. One thing is certain: the Dutch have always had to be inventive, confronted as they were with the task of completing Creation in a land of wind and water, but very few natural comforts. Add to that the fact that the Dutch are born with a quasi-sentimental ideal of resistance (against Spanish, French and German oppressors) and the fact that everyone believes in a slightly different God, and the choice

---

BOLLARDS REPLACED WITH 'DETECTION LOOPS'

AMSTERDAM. **Amsterdam's canals are to be fitted with a new detection system to combat illegal parking. The council wants to remove the characteristic bollards from the canals, but this will once again make it possible for drivers to park their cars on the pavement. A test will therefore be held along the Lauriersgracht, in which electronic loops will be built into the road surface. These will register illegally parked cars and send out an alert to nearby police.**

is clear. Accept chaos, or forge compromises until everyone is blue in the face. The latter solution has become second nature.

No wonder then that the façade of tolerance so often conceals a reality of indifference. The natural inclination to conform, however, keeps it from ever becoming excessive. That is a disadvantage when one cares about originality and individualism, but extremely effective in terms of organisation. At the end of the 1980s, a number of people read somewhere that checked trousers made you look cheerful and relaxed. Within months, several hundred thousand Dutch men between the ages of 30 and 65 had become proud owners of checked leisurewear trousers. Conformist nonchalance allows us to manage the unmanageable in that overcrowded experiment called the Netherlands.

Every country has its own tricks for dealing with public impotence. Let us hope that 'gedogen' does not suffer the same fate as apartheid, for tolerance is something to be treasured. Sometimes it results from principle, but more often it is simply the only solution that doesn't unduly delay business as usual. The Dutch have always been a practical people. They even tolerated president Chirac in his crusading heyday, when he was high on intolerance.

FOREIGNERS IN HOLLAND,
ON HOLLAND

What do the foreigners who live and work in Holland actually think of this country? Writers, managers, scientists and diplomats from all parts of the world – except for Holland – take the floor.

That's the way we do it here

Ethel Portnoy

Like some people who claim they were born in the wrong body, I decided early in life that I had been born in the wrong place: I felt I really belonged in Europe. For the past thirty years I have lived in Holland, which in my opinion is the closest humanity has come to creating heaven on earth with the rather faulty material at hand.

There are many things about the Dutch that suit my personality. Like them I am sober, practical and frugal. Alas, unlike me, they are prone to somber fits; they lack frivolity and a sense of style; they can be blunt or heavy-handed – and that's only the women! But joking aside, despite these minor failings they have managed to create a country where life is very pleasant.

How about fitting in? To become Dutch it's not enough to speak the language fluently, ride a bicycle and hang a birthday-calendar on the door of the wc. Foreigners are welcomed and made to feel at home to the extent that they have pale skins and come from countries with a Judaeo-Christian background. With all others, the Dutch try to be friendly, but their efforts at being multicultural seem forced.

Having grown up in the usa, it's hard for me to understand this. The usa took unto itself all kinds of economic migrants, asylum-seekers and even human garbage. Once such folk are naturalised, they are instantly considered to be one's fellow-Americans. But this atmosphere of immediate acceptance is not present in Holland – nor, to be fair, does one find it in many other European countries. Perhaps because their citizens carry in their hearts the weight of centuries of national history – and often a dark history at that. Or perhaps because they don't feel that their countries contain the limitless space and boundless opportunities one can find in the USA.

Despite the many decades I have spent as a citizen of the Netherlands, as far as I'm concerned the honeymoon between us still isn't over. Yet all honeymoons must eventually end with one coming down from Cloud Nine. Since I am a Dutch citizen – and thus have every right to do so – I should like to point to a number of things in the Netherlands that sometimes cause me to raise my eyebrows. No doubt, in my views on them, I still reflect the impact of my upbringing in the land of the free and the home of the brave.

One of the things that makes me pause is the sentencing practices of Dutch judges. (There are no juries in Dutch

---

LEEUWARDEN POLICE CRITICISED

LEEUWARDEN. **City councillors from the Liberal VVD party in Leeuwarden claim that the police failed to maintain public order on Tuesday night after the football match between local club Cambuur and Excelsior from Rotterdam. According to the councillors, the police did nothing to stop about a hundred hooligans from turning Cambuur Square into a kind of 'free state for vandalism', causing tens of thousands of guilders worth of damage to shops and cars.**

courts.) A schoolgirl who recently pushed one of her class-mates under a train was sentenced to a number of hours of community service. The victim's family must feel some out-rage at this. What happened to the notion of retribution? Shouldn't the punishment fit the crime? Yet in a way I can un-derstand the reasoning of the court when it says in essence: Go thou, and sin no more. The culprit is not a hardened criminal. She will probably not make a career of pushing peo-ple under trains, so she will not be a danger to the communi-ty. Yet she will never be allowed to forget her deed. The op-probrium she encounters will be punishment enough. Only in a small country like this – really a kind of village – can such reasoning be applied.

But this case is a reflection in miniature of what happens in Holland on a wider scale, when questions of punishment or even simple prosecution arise. Time and again in the past few years my jaw has dropped as I have watched corrupt or in-competent officials step down after their misdeeds have been found out, without having to face prosecution, as high Dutch functionaries are not even brought to book for gambling with public funds. Compared to the United Kingdom, libel suits here are more or less laughed out of court, and damages for medical malpractice are derisory.

As for Dutch politics, they seem to me to be a hotbed of cronyism. In the USA, most government officials are elected – here mayors and judges are appointed, governors of prov-inces are parachuted into cushy positions as a reward for service to their parties. The plum jobs are handed out by the parties themselves. When voting, the people are allowed to make their preference for some party clear, after which the party takes over and distributes the spoils. Of course old-boy networks exist in the USA as well (Gore Vidal has told us plen-ty about this); in the USA it takes money to get elected, often big money, and officials may therefore be tempted to sell out to their economic masters. Once in office, elected officials can turn corrupt: look at the mayors of Chicago in the past.

But in the USA the electoral wheel turns every once in a while, and at least there the public feels it can occasionally take a hand in its own fate.

As for real scandals, I've seen them hushed up time and again. The Dutch even have a phrase for this kind of process – putting the affair in the *doofpot*, the way one pushes a firebrand into a barrel of sand. They use this phrase a lot, for they seem to need it frequently.

The Netherlands is famous for being a society that runs on consensus; it is even praised for this, but far less praise or attention is directed at this habit they have of smoothing over unpleasantness. Occasionally a parliamentary committee will be set up to investigate some matter and apportion blame. After which nothing happens. The aim is to keep society running quietly and on an even keel. The Dutch have a saying: *Zo zijn onze manieren* – that's the way we do things. Why rock the boat? For the time being the *doofpot* policy seems to be working, as the citizens of the Netherlands live on in their comfortable, happy snooze.

Born in the USA, Ethel Portnoy came to Europe in 1950. She publishes her writing in Dutch in the Netherlands.

Rushing the homework

Margot Poll

The library at the Mexican embassy houses several hundred books on a broad range of subjects, from culture and politics to economics and foreign affairs. There is only one book on the Netherlands though, a special issue of the magazine *Auge* from 1986. It was a present from the publisher, judging by the note: 'This will no doubt be of interest to you.'

The Mexican Consul, Alicia Pizano, did not even know of the publication's existence. She is the proud owner of a much more beautiful book about the Netherlands, she says, showing off *Los Patines de Plat*, a translation of *Hans Brinker or The Silver Skates*, written by the American author Mary Mapes Dodge in 1865. Pizano received it from her parents on her ninth birthday. She dug it up again when she was informed four years ago that her next posting would be to the Netherlands. Now she reads it to her son, and together they laugh at unpronounceable names such as Geertje, Geurtje or Krelis.

She prepared for her mission in other ways as well. She bombarded her colleagues in The Hague with questions about the country. Are you happy over there? All the answers she received were positive. The streets were safe, the shops sold everything imaginable, pollution was low and it was child-friendly. The people, however, were very different from Mexicans. More serious, friendly only once you got to know them. Pizano says that 'although my first impressions were positive, it was initially more difficult than we had thought. We couldn't find a house, so we stayed in a hotel, then a furnished flat in Scheveningen, before finally moving to a house in Mariahoeve because we insisted on having a garden.' Pizano says she would urge newcomers to find a house before bringing over their family.

German diplomat Peter Dettmar had no such problems. He knew the Netherlands well from frequent holidays in the past. He has been here for four years and loves it, partly because it is so different from his own country. His posting to The Hague came as a complete surprise. The informal list of vacancies that German diplomats are shown annually did not include the job of press attaché in The Hague. When he was asked, though, everything was arranged within half an hour. His wife and young children were immediately enthusiastic, says Dettmar, who has worked in the foreign service for twenty years, including postings to Brussels and West Africa, 'All the aspects of the move were positive – we were all in agreement.'

He spent most of the eight weeks he was given to prepare

POLICE WANT TO SCREEN NEW RESIDENTS

AMSTERDAM. The Chief of Police in Flevoland, G. Horstmann, wants new residents in the province to be screened using police registers from their previous place of residence. In his New Year's speech, he said that newcomers should be screened to pick out troublemakers, and that the information should be used to supplement the database that the Flevoland police already have about 'problem families that produce juvenile delinquents'.

his transfer sorting out the administrative details. As it turned out, his previous experience of the Netherlands as a holiday destination had not prepared him for daily reality. Dettmar, 'It made me very uncertain at first. The politics you read about while on holiday are very different to real-life politics. In fact, Dutch and German politics differ more than I'd thought. German political culture is confrontational and polemic, while Dutch politicians are always looking to form a consensus.'

'Two cultures, two values' is a daily experience for the Chinese Ambassador in The Hague, Hua Liming. 'Of course our nations think and act differently. But no diplomat can properly prepare for that. I was unprepared for the Dutch attitude to China's policy on human rights. I'm always prepared to explain how it works, however: what the differences are, but also how we can bridge the two different cultures. In any case, I prefer dialogue to confrontation.'

Hua Liming had no preparation for his stay in the Netherlands at all, except an hour-long conversation with the Dutch Ambassador to the United Arab Emirates, where Hua had himself been ambassador for two years. His Dutch colleague told him 'everything' about the Netherlands. Homework in a rush, he laughs. He read a number of books, but did not get to know the country until he got here. His wife was very enthusiastic about the transfer to The Hague. No more veil. Arab religious values had not been easy for her, and all the social activities had passed her by. As a woman and a wife, she was never invited to such occasions.

The Netherlands was like a breath of fresh air to them. His wife was allowed to accompany him when he went to present his credentials to the Queen at Noordeinde Palace. They visited Amsterdam on 30 April, and will never forget what they saw. 'How impressed I was! I love this very special way of celebrating the Queen's birthday. That's Dutch culture: very practical, very Dutch.'

Dutch weather is less popular. When Khadija Al-Lawati

came to the Netherlands in November 1999 as ambassador of the much more liberal Gulf state of Oman, she had promised her children snow. It didn't come, only rain. 'We like rain, because we don't get it. Sometimes we held up our hands to catch the rain, to take it to Oman, hoping that perhaps some sun from our country would in turn come over. I've told the children that if it doesn't snow this year, I'll take them to Switzerland or Austria. After all, I had promised them snow when I told them we'd be going to the Netherlands.'

Al-Lawati brought her four children, but her husband stayed behind in Oman. He is advisor to the Minister of Social Affairs, and does not want to abandon his career unless something comparable materialises in the Netherlands. She shrugs her shoulders. She supports her husband's decision, and he supports hers. 'We come from a country where men and women are given equal opportunities. Our Sultan is highly educated and open-minded, just as your Queen is. That is why living in Holland is not difficult for us. My husband comes over every month, and my youngest daughter especially likes that; she misses her father and her cousins very much.'

Once in the Netherlands, diplomats generally gain their footing with the help of colleagues who have been here longer, and with the help of neighbours and, after a while, Dutch friends. On arrival, the Foreign Ministry hands out *The Protocol Guide: Your Posting to the Netherlands*. It provides information related to their diplomatic status – such as tax-free cars, personnel, and diplomatic immunity – but says nothing about actual life in the Netherlands. 'We can answer all their questions about the Netherlands,' says a spokesman from the Cabinet and Protocol Office, 'but only in an informal context. Our main function is as a kind of registry office: we register and hand out official documents.'

Alicia Pizano is still grateful for the help she received from her neighbours in her first week here. When she first went shopping, she was shocked at how expensive everything was.

When she returned home, she started wondering how life could really be quite that expensive. She took her receipt to her neighbour, who spotted the problem immediately. The supermarket had charged her for 300 bottles of milk. An innocent mistake, apparently.

Margot Poll is an editor at NRC *Handelsblad*.

Very blunt in meetings

Marcella Breedeveld

Endless meetings, circulars dealing with yet more new proposals, incessant informal get-togethers round the coffee
machine. Foreign managers starting out in the Netherlands
have a great deal to get used to, not the least of which is the
deep-rooted culture of consensus that dominates many organisations. Decisions are never taken at once. Rather, they
are prepared during a process that may take months, in which
almost everyone gets their say. 'The major criticism of foreign employees is the large number of meetings,' says Jaap
Vossestein, course leader with the Royal Institute for the
Tropics (KIT) and author of the book *Dealing with the Dutch*.
'For heaven's sake, let's stop talking and do something!' an
American participant in one of his courses once cried out.
'Why the Dutch lust for meetings? This love of consensus
and compromise?'

Vossestein's explanation sounds simple: 'This is a country
of minorities. No one group is large enough or dominant
enough to impose its will on another. Negotiation is needed
before anything can be achieved.' At the same time, what initially surprises foreigners most is that the culture of many
minorities leads the Dutch to be very vocal in expressing
their opinions on everything. 'If people don't clearly bring
forward their ideas, preferably backed up with sound argu-
ment, none of these ideas will appear in the final decision. So
opinions are expressed, loudly and clearly, especially if they

do not concern private emotional matters. And one had better not give in until the final decision arrives,' Vossestein writes in his book.

The Dutch don't like veiled language or beating about the bush, as British businessman John Wilkinson can testify. He has worked for three years at the headquarters in The Hague of the Dutch insurance company Aegon. He is an asset manager for pension funds. Most of his business colleagues are foreigners, although his direct colleagues are Dutch. They speak Dutch among themselves, while meetings are normally conducted in English. 'People here are very direct, which sometimes makes them come over as being very blunt in meetings,' says Wilkinson. Not that is matters to him, 'You simply have to bear in mind that some things are typically Dutch.'

Despite the fact that the majority of Aegon's sales are generated abroad, Wilkinson is one of only a handful of foreigners at the head office in The Hague. According to Peter van Os, Vice-President of Human Resources, Aegon has deliberately opted to maintain a small central office that affords a large degree of independence to the various national organisations around the world. As a result of this, expatriates rarely move from one national organisation to another. That is certainly true of Wilkinson. After working as an asset manager for a company in London, he made a conscious decision to send applications to a number of Dutch insurance companies, including Aegon. He wanted to work abroad, and the Dutch pensions market – currently undergoing rapid change – offered the prospect of an attractive working environment.

Those coming to work in the Netherlands are faced with many changes besides their new job. They need to find a house and, if they have children, a school. There are also more bureaucratic things to take care of, such as a bank account, registration with the municipal population register and applying for a 'Sofi-number'. Some multinationals, like Unilever and Shell, employ their own people to take over many of these hassles. Aegon is one of those companies that prefers to leave this to specialised outside agencies. And of course there are also companies, especially in the IT sector, who buy expensive foreign expertise and feel that their responsibility ends with the payment of salaries.

Sanjay Khosla and Jan Droegemueller both came to the Netherlands for Unilever a number of months ago. They are both equally pleased with how the company assisted them in the process of sorting out the social situation. In the words of Indian-born Khosla: 'There is interesting work to be found everywhere, but a foreign posting can quickly turn into a nightmare if your family isn't happy.' He has worked for Unilever in various countries in the last twenty years, and is now Senior Vice-President of Beverages. His previous posting was in England, but he has noticed few differences between the two countries on a professional level. 'This really is a global job. I travel more than half the time. I don't have to learn Dutch; everyone at this level speaks English.'

In private life, however, both Khosla and Droegemueller say, things are rather different. Droegemueller is still rather surprised at this, even though he comes from neighbouring Germany. He had, for example, never expected to find so many differences in regulations between the two countries.

INFLUX OF FOREIGNERS

ROTTERDAM. **According to projections by the CBS (Central Statistics Office), the number of inhabitants of foreign origin will more than double over the next fifteen years, from 800,000 to 2 million. Over this period, the total population of the Netherlands will increase by the same 1.2 million.**

Now that everything has been dealt with, he can afford to laugh. 'There is a lot of bureaucracy in Germany as well, but even that is nothing compared to the number of rules and procedures they have over here.'

Companies like Shell and Unilever, who have been dispatching people all over the world for decades, know better than anyone how much more productive a happy employee is. They have therefore established extensive networks for partners (mostly women, although the number of men is increasing), not only for social contacts but also for exchanging practical information. When a foreign employee comes to the Netherlands to become acquainted with his new working environment, the partner is invited as well. Unilever then ensures that the couple can inspect a number of potential homes during their visit, taking into account, where necessary, such factors as schools or local entertainment. 'I'm rarely home,' says Khosla, 'so it doesn't really matter to me. But, for the same reason, it's very important to me to know that my wife and children are happy.'

Most expatriates leave after three or four years. Their image of the Netherlands is based on contacts at work, their children's school and their neighbours. Almost all are very positive about their neighbours. Despite all the scare stories about growing individualism in Dutch society, it turns out that neighbours can still be vital friends and allies. Given the shortness of their stay, the expats are not in a position to comment on whether the Netherlands – partly as a result of the increasing number of foreign workers – is undergoing change.

But, according to Jaap Vossestein at the Tropics Institute, that change is happening nevertheless. His students increasingly less complain about the slowness of decision-making in companies. They remain critical about the level of service in the Netherlands when it comes to matters such as finding a good plumber, but have become noticeably more enthusiastic about the goods on offer in the shops. And, of course, everyone speaks English, from the man at the grocery store to the girl at the post office.

'Some expats used to regard a posting to the Netherlands as a trip to a penal colony,' Vossestein concludes. 'That's no longer the case.'

Marcella Breedeveld is an editor at NRC *Handelsblad*.

Dutch students talk too much

Sheila Kamerman

On the phone, Professor Alexander Lichtenstein sounds as though he is in a hurry. He is late for another one of those boring meetings. 'Do you want to know what the biggest difference is between universities in Russia, Germany and the Netherlands? In the Netherlands, there are so many meetings to attend. When one meeting is over, there's always another one, and then another. I have to go now, could you ring again this evening?'

No one knows how many foreign academics work at Dutch universities. Not even Nuffic, the organisation responsible for co-ordinating international co-operation in higher education. They do know that the number is low. According to Nuffic spokesman Han van der Horst, the Netherlands is not the most popular destination for academics. They tend to prefer London, Paris or Berlin. 'Not so much because higher education is better there, but because the Netherlands is relatively unknown. Moreover, we don't have top institutes such as Harvard, Yale or the Massachusetts Institute of Technology (MIT). These obviously attract the greatest number of first-class foreign academics.'

Van der Horst suspects that when foreign academics do choose a Dutch university, it is usually because of a suitable vacancy. 'In addition, there are refugees with academic aspirations, such as the former Chilean ambassador Jorge Tapia who used to be Professor of Constitutional Law at the

Erasmus University in Rotterdam.'

For Lichtenstein, born in Russia in 1955 and Professor of Computative Materials Science at the Catholic University of Nijmegen since 1999, the move to a Dutch university was a greater culture shock than it would have been for a Western European. Even those from neighbouring countries, however, must get used to the peculiarities, rules, traditions and etiquette of the Dutch academic world.

Lichtenstein spent seven years as a researcher at the Max Planck Institute in Germany after getting his degree in Russia. He is therefore in a good position to draw comparisons between Dutch, German and Russian universities. Besides the enormous number of meetings that academics in the Netherlands have to attend, Lichtenstein notes that the relationship between students and staff is noticeably more informal. 'In Germany, it would be Herr Professor; here, they like to address you by your first name.' Compared to their German and Russian counterparts, he considers students in the Netherlands to be 'relaxed'.

'Russian students have to pass tough entrance exams to get a place at the top universities. Once they've passed, they're very motivated. The professor is like a God for them, the fountain of all knowledge.' Lichtenstein quickly noticed that Dutch students were very different in this respect. 'They don't respect you just for being a professor. You have to earn their respect. If they disagree with something, they tell you. That took some getting used to at first, but now I've grown to appreciate the feedback.'

The independent-mindedness of Dutch students was also immediately apparent to Franz Palm (1948), Dean of the Economics Faculty at the University of Maastricht. He studied and subsequently taught at the Catholic University of Louvain in Belgium. He has worked in the Netherlands since 1977, first at the Free University in Amsterdam and, since 1985, in Maastricht. 'No one in Belgium would dream of interrupting the professor. Here, they have no qualms about butting in right in the middle of a lecture.'

He also points out the difference in Dutch university curricula. 'Students in Maastricht are incapable of listening to overly theoretical exposés. It soon became obvious that, in order to keep their attention, I had to infuse my lectures with lots of practical examples. Belgian students are exposed to theoretical education in secondary school, where the emphasis is very much on the transfer of knowledge. The Dutch secondary education system is much more skills-based, and the result is apparent at university.'

In Palm's view, Belgian universities place a much greater emphasis in producing well-rounded individuals. 'Economics students also have to pass exams in subjects such as sociology, philosophy and psychology. The same goes for other courses. Dutch university courses tend to be more specialised, even in the first few years.'

Palm is also surprised at the role of the Dutch government in higher education, particularly the frequent modernisation drives initiated by the Education Ministry. 'Even before a project is completed, they come up with another. As a result, the academic community isn't really motivated to participate fully. They don't put a great deal of energy in to it, because they know that it will all be different again in a couple of years' time.' The Belgian government is much less inclined to modernise. 'Change generally comes from the universities themselves, which also means that staff members are generally more enthusiastic about those changes.'

Geoffrey Underhill (1959) is Professor of International Governance at the Political Science Faculty of the University of Amsterdam (UvA). He is very impressed by another aspect of government involvement: the funding of higher education and research. In his first year at the university, he has not had to worry about money. Before coming to the Netherlands, Underhill did research at universities in Canada, England and Scotland. 'For each research project, the first questions were always: "What is it going to cost, and

ACADEMY BOYCOTTS SERBIAN STUDENT

ARNHEM. **The Serbian student Jelena Dadic has been refused enrolment by the Academy of Civil Engineering in Arnhem. Director John Carp was not willing to accept a student born in a country that severely represses a group of people. What annoyed Carp most was that the Serbian did not mention the war in her letter of application. 'She has got quite a nerve,' he concluded.**

where are we going to get the funding?" In the Netherlands, the money is simply there.'

Underhill feels that solid government funding is the only stable foundation for a good system of higher education. 'It's a fact of life that research is very expensive. But you can only attract good researchers if you offer good facilities. More often than not, the best researchers are also the best lecturers.' That is why he will continue to encourage his Dutch colleagues to protest again further funding cuts. 'Nevertheless, in comparison to other countries where I've worked, they have no idea how good their position currently is.'

He also appreciates the influence that students have on the day-to-day running of the university. They take part in university and faculty committees which discuss education and research, and are therefore able to hold up a mirror to the staff members. 'Their criticism helps us make improvements. In England, the situation is totally different. Some lecturers get upset at the very idea of being criticised by students.'

Underhill is less enthusiastic about the – in his view –

excessive freedom students are afforded in the Netherlands. 'They do four-year courses, but they're all still there after five years.' He is also surprised at the number of exam retakes on offer to students. 'No other country I know affords such luxury. If you fail an exam at a Canadian university, you simply choose another subject and try to pass that. If you fail that, you have to redo the whole year. Obviously, it's more expensive for the taxpayer. Perhaps the money might be better spent on hiring more staff and decreasing class sizes.'

It may sound strict, but Underhill considers these useful lessons. Universities should not merely pass on specific knowledge; their task is also to prepare their students for later life. Students must learn to deal with deadlines, commitments and stress. That still leaves more than enough time to have fun.

Sheila Kamerman is an editor at NRC *Handelsblad*.

Being from Barcelona

Sarah Hart

One day I shall write a novel about foreigners living in Holland. Like Anthony Burgess's book set in Rome, where people who had scaled the innumerable flights of stairs to the top floor had to lie down, gasping for breath (books and magazines were supplied until they were able to speak), there will be one running joke throughout; every time anybody steps outside he will be narrowly missed by a cyclist, who whizzes by on the pavement, shouting rude words at him.

These contacts with cyclists, however glancing, do wonders for one's vocabulary, and their righteously contorted faces and raised middle fingers could go straight into Desmond Morris's book of typical national gestures. It is probably the first thing foreigners notice about this country – and could very easily be the last – and the most frightening thing about it is the self-control needed not to do it oneself. I don't swear, yet, but I have definitely developed the same reluctance to stop once I get on my bicycle.

There are other habits to be picked up; one that I am proud of is remembering to congratulate parents on their children's birthdays. Husbands and wives are held responsible for each other's birthdays, grandparents for their grandchildren's, probably evil stepmothers too. I was thrown into confusion once by being congratulated on the birthday of my husband's granddaughter; when in doubt it is best to congratulate everyone in sight.

Birthdays are important in Holland. Toddlers in play-groups stagger around the circle of children, offering them chunks of sausage and cheese on their birthdays, in primary school the teacher announces that tomorrow she will be celebrating her birthday and expects a present, people in offices treat each other to cakes on their birthdays, and the only exclusively Dutch public holiday of the year is the Queen's birthday (although it is, like the primary school teacher's, an official birthday, not her real one). On people's birthdays you drop into their house and sit round in a circle, *in de kring*, just like the children at playgroup (and then I always hear the words from Cranford about the circle of chairs: 'the circle around the fire, which reminded me of Stonehenge, I don't know why').

Once there, you get a slice of tart with whipped cream – the sausage and cheese are only for those too small to protest – and a cup of tea so weak that it is no more than water with the faintest memory that a tea-bag was once associated with it. This will be in my novel too, as a useful restorative after a near miss by a cyclist. I once saw seven people served tea from a pot with one tea-bag in it; later more water was added and seven more cups poured. In England you have to wait until six o'clock before having a drink; in Holland, you can start at five, and you can see why, after such a tea.

I have been a foreigner for years now, first in France and now in Holland; after a bit you get the hang of it, despite moments of paranoia. So in France, if you say 'bonjour' to people towards the end of the afternoon, a certain proportion of them will reply 'bonsoir'. To the next person therefore you say, brightly, 'bonsoir', and he replies 'bonjour'. It is exactly the same here: if you say 'dag', people answer 'hallo' and if you try 'hallo' it will be their day for 'dag'.

When this happens I feel like Manuel, the Spanish waiter in *Fawlty Towers*, the one who never understands, who gets everything wrong, yet keeps trying. When he is completely baffled all he can do is say, desperately: '¿Qué?' And then

John Cleese says, 'Don't mind him, he's from Barcelona.' It is exhausting being a foreigner; there you are, doing your best, copying the natives and pretending to understand them, your beliefs shaken to the core every time you say hello to someone. And yet, just as there are Dutch people scattered all over the world, so there are many more foreigners here than you might think. In fact there is a strong chance that in the Stonehenge of chairs at the birthday tea there is at least one other foreigner; I was at a large family gathering here once where only one of the spouses was Dutch – all the rest of us were from Barcelona.

Sarah Hart is Irish. She writes on literary subjects; for ten years she was also gardening correspondent for *NRC* *Handelsblad*.